the oxford diaries

A Student Travelogue

j.a. jernay

foreword

In the spring of 2014, while packing my belongings for a cross-country move, I stumbled across a pair of old leatherbound books, one burgundy, the other forest green. They felt weirdly familiar in my hands.

Then I recognized them. They were my diaries from my time studying abroad at Oxford University.

That night, I poured a glass of wine and cracked open the books and settled in for what I thought would be an embarrassing trip down memory lane. As I turned the pages, I was surprised. These diaries were more than I'd expected.

They were kind of … *good*.

Certainly not perfect. Parts were out of chronology, other parts lacked structure, a few events were missing entirely. It was what you would expect from a smart teenager handwriting the first draft of a travelogue in pen, legally drinking alcohol for the first time.

Going to Oxford University had been my first journey abroad, my first step out of the Midwest nest. I had clearly been swinging for the fences, writing-wise.

Of course, keeping a handwritten diary in a leatherbound journal did seem a little antiquated at the time. My only explanation is that it somehow must have felt right to follow the old ways there, at the third-oldest university in the world. I was probably thinking that if J.R.R. Tolkien and C.S. Lewis and Oscar Wilde and a thousand other luminaries of the Oxford literary world could write their genius works by hand, then so would I.

I'm one hundred percent American, but you'll notice more than a few archaic British expressions in these diaries. Reading them today, it feels like someone trying on a Victorian smoking jacket and spinning in front of a mirror, trying to decide how it looks. I let the language stand, but you can trust that words such as *jolly, doughty, nary, chap, splendiferous,* etc. wouldn't stand a chance against my editing pencil today.

Those romantic months at Oxford seem to have influenced me in other ways too. There, I learned about Francis Bacon and the *Novum Organum,* his aborted attempt to chronicle all human knowledge through empiricism. At the time, I laughed at that project, joked about it with friends, dismissed it as the silly fantasy of a megalomaniac.

Today I can sheepishly admit that my own ambitions have taken me along the same path, kind of. What kind of person decides to write an ongoing series of adventure mystery novels about *every country in the entire world*? Seriously—who *does* that? Me, apparently.

Today, Ainsley Walker, Cosmo Bennett, and all my other investigator protagonists serve as my vehicle of exploration, but their roots can be found here at Oxford University, my first foreign adventure.

J.A. Jernay

september 1

. . .

THE IMMIGRATION ROOM at London Gatwick was
unnaturally still. A stern woman behind a tall yellow desk
took my passport and matched my face to my photo. She
didn't seem to like the fact that I didn't have a firm return
flight booked, but the formal letter from Dr. Finlay, my new
principal at Oxford University, got me through nonetheless.

Outside at the bus depot, I recognized another student
from the airplane and introduced myself. It turned out that he
was headed for Oxford University too, and was even in my
program, so we accompanied each other on the coach.

He didn't have much to say, so I spent the next two hours
staring silently out the window. As the coach motored along
the rural roads, I was surprised to see that American busi-
nesses have festered across the British landscape. Mobil to the
left, Texaco to the right. Even the gaping maw of a Safeway
anchored what could only be described as—*dum da DUM dum*
—a strip mall. In many areas it was indistinguishable from
Arlington, Virginia.

Except for the cars. America is the home of the big automobile, gas-gulping yellow Cadillacs with steer horns on the

hood. Here is different. Tiny Citroëns and Peugots putter about the streets like covered riding lawn mowers.

The street signs are understandable. Only one stumped me: *Begin free recovery* is posted before freeway construction, and *End free recovery* afterwards. How does *free recovery* mean *construction*? It boggles the Yank mind. But top prize for the weirdest street sign goes to *humped zebra crossing*, which I figured out meant crosswalk.

We arrived at Keble College, where I'm enrolled in a special program for study-abroad students. It has its own building a short distance away, in the bustling commercial heart of Oxford. I checked in, got my room assignment, and crashed upon my short but comfortable bed for two hours. My body clock was feeling the effects of the transatlantic redeye.

I awoke to the sound of two familiar voices in the hallway. It was Sabina and Catherine, two friends from my home university. The three of us were the chosen emissaries to Oxford University this year. Sabina is a tall blonde who turns heads wherever she goes, but her genteel Southern manners keep her extremely nice. She carries her favorite salad dressing wherever she goes because, in her words, "you never know".

At five pm, there was a reception for all new students in the lounge. There I met the esteemed Dr. Finlay. He's exactly the way I had imagined. He peers at you over his bifocals, and through his graying teeth issues a fast-flowing river of *veddy* British intellectual conversation. He's an arrogant but charming man. The rumor says that he was friends with John Cleese when they were both undergraduates, and that they performed the Ministry of Funny Walks together. It probably benefits him to let the rumor continue.

Before night fell, I stepped out of the college and took a stroll that proved less than pleasant. The reason: Traffic in Oxford is horrendous. Gnarls and unpredictable backups make it a test of one's courage to even cross the street. Looking to the right (unlike the U.S., where we look to the left) doesn't guarantee safety because there are so many one-way streets that cars can fly from either direction.

Most importantly, on my walk, I found the Eagle and the Child. I didn't enter just yet. The first day is too soon. There will be time.

september 2

. . .

INDEED THERE WAS TIME. It's my second day, and I've just returned from The Eagle and the Child. I spent two hours in the famous back room, where J.R.R. Tolkien and C.S. Lewis and others met every Tuesday morning from the nineteen-thirties to the nineteen-sixties. They were part of a group of intellectual but popular writers known as the Inklings. It was in this pub that Lewis first read aloud chapters from his new book about children walking through a magic wardrobe into a make-believe world.

My companions were other study-abroad students. A pleasant, offbeat Allen Ginsberg fan named Alexandra. A handless farmboy from Nebraska named Adam who avoided explaining his unfortunate condition. An enormously tall Swedish brunette named Gerda whose English was good enough to spit the Peter Piper tongue twister right back at me. "My name is *not* Inga," she added, "and I don't wear blonde pigtails under a Viking helmet."

Then we were joined by one of our professors, Dr. Gordon Cox-Davies. He's a short, jolly don who doubles as a tour guide. He lifted a pint of beer above our table and spoke movingly of its golden-brown color and warm (55° Farenheit) temperature. "It slides down the throat without touching either side," he said.

We all toasted one another. Except for a few terrible bottles of Coors, I haven't really drunk beer before. I'm not legal yet in the U.S. This stuff is really good, at least in Oxford, and several people have said that we're going to get spoiled here.

I ambled through Christ Church Meadow later in the afternoon. Founded by Cardinal John Wolsey, Christ Church is the most prestigious college at Oxford. Oscar Wilde, Lewis Carroll, King Edward VII, and even Dudley Moore all passed through its gates. The history here is palpable, it sends chills down my spine, and I'm not even an Anglophile like my sister.

St. Giles Fair will be revving up tomorrow for two days. No different from any municipal carnival in the U.S., it attracts rapscallions, ne'er-do-wells, and "people of dubious moral standards," according to Dr. Cox-Davies. The social dangers seem to be exaggerated here. We've already been subjected to a lecture by another don, Dr. Timothy Brown, about the importance of avoiding religious cults while at Oxford. Curious, I raised my hand and asked what awful activities these cults engaged in. He answered, very seriously, that they hold prayer sessions and visit sick people in hospitals but that "nonetheless they will take your body and mind and hold it captive". Part of me wonders if, by that definition, half of the people in my country qualify as members of religious cults.

There've been a few problems so far. The electric sockets don't seem to be accepting my $34.95 Radio Shack 220-volt converter. And the showers are temperamental. I finally folded and ran a nice steaming hot bath. It was relaxing and I've vowed to do it more often.

I took dinner at another historic pub, The King's Arms. I imagine it got its name during the English Civil War, but I don't know for sure. It's really popular with students, and the meat pie was deeply satisfying. I know it sounds weird, given its bad reputation, but I actually *like* British food so far. Maybe because much of it is Americanized. In the grocery store this morning, I noticed many familiar items, from Cinnamon Toast Crunch to Campbell's Soup. Even Pizzaland, my restaurant of choice last night, was possessed of a Chuck E. Cheese atmosphere. America is truly the world's cultural dominatrix.

At least for now.

september 4

· · ·

LECTURES STARTED TODAY. First up was Boethius' transmission of learning from Greek into Latin. Interesting enough to keep half my attention. If I hadn't already had two intense years of humanities classes to build up my tolerance to hardcore scholarship, I probably would've passed out from boredom.

The Westgate Public Library, two short blocks away, has accepted my application. It's pretty decent for a public library —this is Oxford, after all—but the author and title catalogues are on microfiche.

I was out rambling today, looking for a bank to accept me. None did. This is worrisome, because I have an enormous cashier's check that isn't cashing itself. It's all my spending money for the trip. Annoyed, I ducked down a cobblestone alley and randomly fell into a dark pub called the Wheat-sheaf. I pulled up a stool and watched as a bowl of steak-and-kidney stew, a flaky bun, and a plate of peas were hand-delivered to my rough-hewn table. It was solid food. As I chewed, a small plaque over the lintel caught my eye, particularly the cheery phrase, "We'll teach you to drink deep ere you depart."

I don't want to depart.

september 5

· · ·

IN LECTURE TODAY, Dr. Cox-Davies touted the virtues of Oxford. This city, he said, is the sixth-largest in England, and it was a center of commerce long before it was a college town. Two of the three roads in ancient Saxony passed by either side of it.

He told a funny story about the clash between town and gown. Back in the thirteenth century, the townspeople in Oxford frowned upon the scholars for their laziness. Easy to understand why, since the medieval scholastics were engaging in prolonged debates about how many angels could dance on the head of a pin.

Things reached the breaking point when a scholar decided to practice archery from his bedroom window. He took aim at a basket of apples on the head of a townswoman passing by. He missed and accidentally killed the woman. Enraged, the townspeople rose up and slaughtered half the scholars. Sounds like a drunken dare gone horribly wrong.

The remaining scholars had a choice to make. They could stay in Oxford, where they were hated, or establish a new school, far from the nosy intrusions of the urban populace. A portion of the scholars elected to leave, and they traipsed across the fenlands, where they founded Cambridge University, out in silence and peace.

"And that is why," he said, "Cambridge is on the way to *nowhere.*"

I totally love silly rivalries, and the more ancient, the better.

———

I owe a debt of gratitude to Dr. Finlay. Today, with the weight of his name and with the stern, headmistress tone of Rosie Robertson—the Registrar with a Ramrod up her Rear—I finally have a bank account at Westminster Bank. The bank hadn't wanted to allow a nineteen-year-old from the U.S. to open an account, but the college personally vouched for me. Whew. Now I can buy food again.

I took an oath at the Bodleian Library today. I promised not to "kindle any flames" in the stacks, nor to remove a book from its reading room. My question is this: Why am I swearing fealty to a dead man whose scions won't even allow me to *use* the damn library after October 7, when all the British students—aka "real" students—hit town? Would they have extended my privileges if I had recited the oath in Latin?

The entire Oxford University library system is just as frustrating. It's nearly useless because of inefficiency. The Bodleian has apparently been long abandoned by all *real* scholars who harbor any notions of speedy research. The library at my satellite college is only open for two hours a day, and books take an hour to be removed by somebody who is standing only thirty feet away from them. I'm even told that the Christ Church library still chains its books to the shelves.

september 6

. . .

"THE FACT that the cows are lying down usually indicates that rain is on the way."

Thus spake Dr. Cox-Davies, demonstrating his encyclopedic knowledge of dormant bovines.

It's Wednesday, and we were on our way to Bath for our first weekly field trip to sites of historical interest. Outside the window passed a grass-covered mound, scooped out in the center and hidden behind a clump of trees. Dr. Cox-Davies said that it was an ancient amphitheater constructed in the first century A.D. We also drove through Cotswold, the original cotton village. They say it was a real, ahem, cottage industry.

The baths themselves aren't very impressive: a pool of tepid water surrounded by some reconstructed ruins. I spent most of our time thinking that those who derive the most pleasure from this tour are probably those with the most vivid historical imaginations, the type of people who can easily picture the arched dome collapsing into the pool upon hundred of naked Romans. (A true story, apparently.) Me, I wondered why they still call the place Bath when nobody is allowed to bathe in them. Perhaps it should be renamed Sink, or Faucet, or Trough.

At the end of the tour Dr. Cox-Davies gestured to a glass of greenish-yellow water sitting on a tabletop. That was Bath water, he said, and dared somebody to drink from it. I accepted the dare. How bad could it be? This was supposedly the same restorative water that has lured travelers here ever since the Romans built the entire temple complex and called the springs Aquae Sulis.

I took a huge gulp and put the glass back down. The water was putrid and made me sick.

I felt better later, once some friends and I arrived at the Pulteney Bridge, which spans the River Avon. We had lunch at the Cherry Hill Tea Room, a tiny restaurant located on the bridge directly over the still waters. It was a breezy, crisp afternoon as I feasted on crumpets and jam, red pepper and carrot soup, and garlic bread.

Later, alone, my feet carried me over to the Royal Crescent, an early example of public planning. Then I stumbled upon a game of British bowling, which is played on what we Americans would call a putting green. Teams of geezers in white smocks and gray slacks and skirts rolled small black balls across the grass. The one who lands closest to the white ball wins.

I halfheartedly thought about trying to finding Peter Gabriel too. He lives in Bath, and his record label and studio complex are located somewhere here as well. I did spend a few minutes looking for Mercy Street, but no luck. I swear they moved that sign.

The musician's words are as true in Bath as they are everywhere. *All of these buildings, all of the cars, were once just a dream, in somebody's head.*

september 7

. . .

TODAY WAS the best and worst of times.

A new don, Alastair Lowsley, delivered an excellent lecture on the history of England. He displayed a succession of *waistcoats*, which is the British term for vests, corresponding to the historical era that he was describing. He wore a golden one during the Roman Empire, a dark one during the Dark Ages (a little too on-the-nose), and Scottish plaid during the medieval portion.

The second lecturer, whom I'll only call Piers, put us to sleep, though. A visiting scholar from another college, Piers was incomprehensible. The topic was Bede, and I quickly became convinced that only his podium was going to pass the Bede portion of the exam, because he hunched over it for an entire hour, head down, mumbling and reading notes off yellowed pieces of paper.

Rounds of tequila shots at the Wheatsheaf tonight, followed by a trivia contest. An American bartender named Steve shouted trivia questions at the patrons, who wielded pen and paper. The winners got a free round. Sample question: *What is the actual zip code of Beverly Hills?* Or: *According to reports issued Friday, what is the most economically prosperous country in Europe?* Our resident Viking, Gerda, had no idea of her good fortune and missed the answer: Sweden.

september 8

. . .

STUDIED ALL AFTERNOON AND EVENING. I learned that Chrétien de Troyes' story of the Holy Grail doesn't actually end. It just trails off in mid-sentence. Scholars think he either died or became ghastly ill, because at that point there are fourteen different conclusions written by fourteen different hands.

At eleven-thirty at night, done with reading, I bolted off my bed and went down to Bonn Square for a baked potato with the hungry drunken masses. The square was teeming with people with nowhere else to go because Oxford still clings to a ridiculously early closing time for the pubs—eleven thirty pm. After that, I was brimming with energy, so I began to explore.

Walking down St. Aldate's Street, past Christ Church, I found the River Thames. I walked along its bank for what seemed like forever, in the hopes that I would eventually smack my head upon Magdalen Bridge.

Wrong.

I found myself underneath a wholly unfamiliar freeway. Wanderlust had bitten hard, though, and soon I was leaving trails of smoke from my sneakers.

The southern suburbs of Oxford are really quite ... um, well, they just *are*. Rows upon dreary rows of prefabricated identical houses, much like I imagined the neighborhood in Madeleine L'Engle's *A Wrinkle In Time*. I wandered past an elementary school. Behind it lay soccer fields with a makeshift lean-to made from a cardboard box. It smelled like urine, even from this distance.

Wait a minute. I stopped and did a double take. I had begun my ramble downtown, which is the fancy, sophisticated, mercantilistic part of the city. Now I was in the suburbs. Can it be true that, in Oxford, the police push the homeless *out to the suburbs*? The opposite of the American urban pattern?

I saw several more lean-tos before the night was through.

An hour later, totally lost, I was forced to turn completely around and trace my way back, like Tom Sawyer and Sally in the cave.

september 11

. . .

THIS AFTERNOON, with the energy of a cartoon-hyper, sugared-up toddler, I stepped onto a punt at Magdalen Bridge.

Instead of using that wondrous invention called the paddle, Oxonians have instead opted to retain their reputation for efficiency in all pursuits and furnish their boaters with *poles*. This makes it impossible to push in a straight line. Punts bounce from bank to bank like air hockey disks.

To make a prickly situation even worse, I was pulling the punt from the front—a Cambridge tradition—rather than pushing from the rear in a more Oxford fashion. Such *faux pas*. Alexandra also did my back a great favor by steering me into a nest of picker bushes.

That night we dined on value meals at KFC with Gerda, then met a Paki friend named Shariq who had a couple bottles of cheap Bulgarian wine, added them to our two bottles of cheap stuff, and traipsed down to the Thames. A full moon, a scenic riverbank, four people, four bottles of alcohol. Nothing but lapping water and happy gulping and tinkling laughter.

Then, in a burst of surrealism, a longboat suddenly cut

through the night. It was a party boat sailing down the river, directly before our eyes, from right to left. It carried three hundred brightly-lit partygoers, the drunkest ones hanging off the sides of the boat and whooping like monkeys. "Dancing Queen" by Abba was coming across the water.

Behind the party boat were four teenage boys rowing a skiff in its wake, trying desperately not to lose the party. They saw us, gave up, and paddled over. Docking on the riverbank, they climbed up on the lawn and entertained us for an hour. One taught me the local tradition of punching knuckles together and saying, "Respect!" Another claimed that his older brother's band had just been offered an opening slot for Pearl Jam. Skeptical, I asked for the name, and he said Supergrass. I'd never heard of them. A third told me that my cricket jacket (wool sweater) marks me as a tourist. A fourth one claimed that he wasn't racist because he went to Ireland once.

Finally the boys hopped into the meadow behind us and gamboled about in the bright moonlight like pubescent centaurs.

september 12

. . .

THE KEBLE COLLEGE dining hall has to be seen to be believed.

It's a grand wooden room with tradition seeping out of the walls. To enter, you have to be wearing the traditional black gown. There are no seats, only long wooden benches that take at least three people to pull out, so everybody sits down for dinner together and stands up to leave together. The dons have a special high table on a dais, and we have to stand when they enter the room.

Dinner is served at seven o'clock every evening, usually pork, potatoes, vegetables, and a roll. You can buy soup for 25 pence extra, which I always do, even though it's just broth. Dessert is something really sweet and thick, like rum cake with clotted cream poured all over it. I'm eating a lot but somehow still losing weight. It might be because trying to talk to my fellow diners is impossibly stressful. The Keble College students usually pretend that I don't exist. I think that the traditional English class system is so firmly lodged in their minds that it precludes the idea of ever conversing with an American. To them, I'm some strange, cheerful, dancing monkey with zero approach anxiety, the type of dangerously open-hearted character who is better avoided in the name of God and Queen.

I haven't made a British friend yet.

Later this afternoon, I wrangled on the phone with the manager of the First of America branch back home. He was being obstinate and suddenly travelers' checks began to look very attractive once again. Later, as I hurried nervously about the building in a faxing frenzy, I was calmed down by Dr. Finlay, whose arrogant attitude belies an essentially good nature.

"Don't get so pent up about these little things," he said. "They don't mean anything. It'll sort out."

We proceeded to chat a bit more about everything from Oxford prodigies ("they tend to be in math") to the problem of prodigies and pubs ("their intelligence usually protects them from the town") to the link between scientific and musical minds ("Einstein loved playing his violin at parties, much to the chagrin of others").

My last thought is a random analogy: Parents are like fine china. They've been in the house forever, they were given to you by their parents, and the older they are, the more likely they are to have floral patterns.

september 13

. . .

THE IRONY. After agreeing with the British bank that I would indeed at last deposit The Check—thousands of dollars, all my spending money for the study-abroad—I find that the bank on this morning alone opens not at 9:00 am, but at 9:30 am. I have to wait even longer. Poetic justice.

Still, deposit made. At long last.

Today was another field trip. On the bus I chatted with Kevin. He's like P.J. O'Rourke, but liberal—tough childhood, no money, deadbeat dad, extreme political views, former drug habit, etc. We agreed that our branch of Keble College was the most openly liberal place we've ever been. That's like manna from heaven for a socialist like him.

The Wells Cathedral is gorgeous, perpendicular, ornate, and breathtaking. It is the first completely Gothic structure in Europe. In 1338, the west side sank three inches, and giant scissor-shaped beams were erected in the transept to support the cracked structure. They look natural.

We literally ducked into a pub at lunch (it had a very low ceiling), only to find Dr. Cox-Davies sipping a tall pint of beer in a corner. He's always doing that, it seems, and it felt totally natural to join him for a pint, even though he's nearly as old as my grandfather. What a jolly country where one can eat, drink, and be merry with one's professor, week after week.

Glastonbury Abbey was a forceful testament to the inevitable return of Nature – she will retake everything that we build, grow, or fence in. The abbey's tall walls stood crumbling against the blue sky; brown tufts of grass and weeds covered their tops and crevices. It reminded me of Thomas Cole's fifth painting in his *Course of the Empire* series. It provides a strong contrast to the splendiferous, doughty spirit of other churches that refuse to let Nature take Her course.

The supposed grave of King Arthur lies between two half-crumbled stone walls. But who really knows if it's him? There's no way to prove it. Probably it's some eleventh-century schmuck wriggling with delight at the oodles of tourists paying respect at his grave. The most noble act he probably performed during his lifetime was to pick lice from his hair *outside* the hut, thank you very much. Nonetheless, like a good tourist, I snapped a couple of photos of the mound of grass. Kodak is responsible for the perpetuation of more questionable history than even the ex-Soviet Union's Ministry of Education.

Next, some of us decided to climb to the Glastonbury Tor, a stone edifice that stands forlornly at the top of a huge barrow, which supposedly has a labyrinth inside that is accessible only through a secret door. I understand now how Tolkien wrote *The Lord of the Rings*, given natural terrain like this. The Tor (which I think inspired Weathertop) also supposedly houses the Holy Grail. Again, color me skeptical.

Alexandra and I paused to pick blackberries along the country road leading by the Tor. We wended our way through grazing sheep and up narrow, winding stairs and finally emerged at the plateau at the summit.

Words are inadequate to describe the view, but more important was the understanding that it gave me. Ascending mountains is a pilgrimage of sorts, a testimonial to the mysterious human need to scamper to the top of large natural formations. We are much more loath to descend into a cavern or trench or fissure. Hopefully this says something positive about human nature.

We passed by Stonehenge on the return trip. How disappointing. You can't walk among the ruins, they're smaller than they would appear to be, and mention of Spinal Tap was nowhere to be found. Still, one can't help but speculate about 5000-year-old ruins erected in the middle of BumbleBrit Nowhere, even back then, and for religiously ceremonial reasons. I have to find a copy of *Chariots of the Gods?*, the widely dismissed yet provocative study of the connection between aliens and ancient ruins.

september 14

. . .

ANOTHER GUEST LECTURER delivered another dry lecture this morning. This one was on the rise of the Capetian Monarchy in France. This lecture was new ground for me, and he spared no details. A typical sentence: "In 1128, Geoffrey, son of Fulk V, married Matilda, daughter of Henry I. Henry died, but Matilda's brother Stephen, king of Jerusalem, returned to claim rightful inheritance..." It went on and on like that, for an hour and a half.

This afternoon I walked through Abingdon Park with Alexandra and Gerda. We picked black raspberries, crossed the Locks of Abingdon on the Thames, got chummy with a pooch named Holly, and were drenched by rain.

We met Gerda's host family's children. Michael, aka Grendel, is really a cute kid. He gave me a Playdough cookie. Gerda says that he has trouble separating Swedish from English—he's only three and a half—and speaks a mutated linguistic conglomeration I've dubbed Swedglish.

His older sister, Jessica, is a doll. She wore a pink ballet dress and skipped through the house with a basket of flowers under her arm like an expatriated Heidi confined to the gray quarters of suburban Oxfordshire. We held hands.

Mother is a concert pianist. The piano in the living room cost fifty thousand pounds.

———

Richard Green is the Keble College junior class president. That's one of those meaningless student government positions that people fight so hard for. *Elect me and I'll add a Mello Yello nozzle in the cafeteria.* He's an angry youth, storming around in a hilarious way, fulminating at this or that. He's also lost most of his hair already, which might explain the anger. I'd be angry if I lost my hair at age twenty-one.

Richard is living here in our building, and after dinner tonight, conversation slid into a big, heated comparison of American vs. British culture. He voiced concern over hard-right Republicans and the Christian Coalition, invoking the name of Ralph Reed. Jokingly, we called him a pinko and asked if he pays *anything* to go to Oxford, or does the government just pick up the entire tab. He told us that Americans were too violent; we told him that the British sense of humor was too dry. That part, at least, wasn't true, for when I asked him for his opinion of the rowing team, he glanced at me and said, "Sadists, complete sadists." He's right. I've learned that the crew team meets for a four-thirty am practice, seven days a week.

september 15

· · ·

HOW TO BECOME AN ALCOHOLIC, In Two Easy Steps:

1. Buy a plane ticket to Oxford, England.
2. Have the luxury of four weeks until your first
   paper is due.

A group of friends met at Bella Pasta, and I ordered
brandy for dessert. My first brandy. Holy cow, I thought that
was a light drink. No wonder mom dilutes it with so many
ice cubes.

We popped into The Bear, Oxford's oldest pub, but the
ceiling was too low and it was too crowded and it made us
feel claustrophobic. We set off for Oddbins, a wine shop.

There I noticed that the Oddbins magazine features
artwork by Ralph Steadman, Hunter S. Thompson's longtime
illustrator. I've always loved his work, so I mentioned his
name to the cashier. A twinkle appeared in his eye, and the
man told me that Steadman demands to be paid only in wine.

Perfect.

september 16

. . .

THIS MORNING, having imbibed enough spirits for quite some time, my besotted mind decided to hit the pavement and soak in the cultural flavor of Oxford. Which, truth be told, tastes a lot like last night's Worthington Best Bitter followed by tequila chasers.

The Ashmolean Museum is pretty much your average collection of prehistoric and historic pots, pans, dishes, bowls, and jugs. It should be named Crockery Through The Ages.

There is quite an extensive collection of Far Eastern statuary, though three hundred brass and iron Buddhas left me looking for the exit of that particular wing.

One room, the Tradescant Exhibit, is filled with slightly more relevant curios from British history—Guy Fawkes' lantern, Henry VIII's gloves, Oliver Cromwell's death mask, and a wooden plate made from the oak tree in which Charles II hid from his Roundhead pursuers. Oddest of all, Powhatan's mantle was on display. He was the father of Pocohontas—or Aerobohontas, to those only familiar with the Disney film.

After passing the mummified Egyptian fish, I turned smack dab into Auguste Rodin's The Thinker. The poor thing is only a foot high. The reproduction in Detroit (which is one of eight, I'm told) is absolutely mammoth, at least three times as big as a person. The Brits might be right on this one—I've never seen any power forwards at Crisler Arena listed as philosophy majors.

Wandered through several of the twenty-five colleges for the remainder of the afternoon. Corpus Christi affords a gorgeous view of Christ Church and its meadow. New College is ironically one of the oldest, dating to 1379, and is surrounded by the original city wall, replete with ramparts. And I experienced a very strong OM (Oxford Moment) as I crouched in a corridor facing Balliol's main quad, a rainstorm hammering the stone and the grass all around me.

september 17

. . .

KATHARINE, Gerda's best friend who is currently living in London, visited for a few hours today. Two Swedes for the price of one. I retraced with them my path of yesterday: Ashmolean, New College, coffee shop, etc. I greatly amused Katharine with my imitation of a drawling Texan being amazed by the sights.

After shoving her onto a bus and being joined by Alexandra, the three of us bummed around on Gloucester Green, a giant brick plaza bordered by modern stores and housing. It quickly became a free-for-all against me: they cut a lock of my hair and tied my shoes together. We ambled and capered around with no particular destination in mind until we found ourselves in the loft of the Oxford Pub and Bakery, where Gerda and I got Alexandra a little stewed by forcing shot after shot of Bailey's down her throat.

After a quick Burger King stop—the Whopper was thoroughly nondescript and that's good because what they're aiming for is consistent mediocrity anyways—we sat by the Thames and sipped tea at the Head of the River.

I feel both happy and anxious about having frittered away the whole day. It's not something I usually do.

september 18

. . .

ANOTHER OM. As I entered the darkened, oaken Keble College library tonight, I heard rain pattering against the high-vaulted ceiling. I was completely alone in this creaky library. A creepy feeling crawled around in my butt. I was compelled by something to sit down under a solitary desk lamp and begin reading about the medieval tradition of courtly love.

It was a tradition of French troubadours for about a century, but its strength was so great that it still today permeates every aspect of our pattern of social relationships. Bringing flowers, opening doors, pulling out the chair, paying for dinner—they can all be traced back to Guinevere and Lancelot. And now the PC squad is itching to stuff all tradition down a well in the name of perfect equalism. That seems vaguely fascist.

It's funny what reading old history can do for your perspective on life.

september 19

. . .

HAD my first bona fide British haircut today. You can choose between a junior stylist, a stylist, and a senior stylist. The caste system dies in India and is reborn in English hair salons. I guess they imported more than just fabrics.

My stylist was sporting, shall we say, a natural underarm look. Seeing a tuft of brown hair curling out from your hair stylist's pits doesn't inspire confidence in her abilities. It's sort of like watching your furniture mover limp up the front walk with thin arms and bony legs.

This afternoon, I toured the famous Oxford Union. It's one of the oldest debating societies in the world, and the buildings have libraries, halls, billiards lounges, and a bar.

Our tour guide was a student from St. John's College. He spoke in rapid spurts of English separated by seconds of silent vocal struggle, like a machine gun seizing up on itself. He seemed very nervous and toyed with his collar. I don't know why, since he's a debater.

He told us about the celebrities who've addressed the Union recently. Apparently Imran Khan, cricket player extraordinaire and wannabe Pakistani politician, spoke last year. Kermit the Frog appeared the year before that. Billy Joel performed a three-hour concert, mixed with a question-and-answer session, before a packed house of one thousand. That's probably the smallest room he's played to in a while.

Seven prime ministers have been officers of the Union. Richard Nixon gave his first post-Watergate lecture there. William Gladstone and Benazir Bhutto have been its president. This year, on October 3, the famous intellectual Dan Quayle is coming to speak. And they're working on another top political figure in the American political scene for November. If it turns out to be Newt, I'm going to invest in a bullhorn.

Rowan Atkinson was a Union member and blames his less-than-spectacular marks on the two fabulous snooker tables on the second floor.

Near the end of the tour, we entered a vast, book-lined library, I saw an elderly man relaxing in a thick leather chair in the corner. His shoes were off, and his brown Argyles had a hole in the big toe. He was snoozing with his mouth open.

Another OM.

september 20

. . .

FOR TODAY'S weekly field trip, we visited Warwick Castle. It proved to be the best part of the course thus far. The State Rooms are ancient and lavishly decorated—the Dining Hall can be rented out for 7000 pounds per night. Portraits of Charles II, Henry VIII, and his various mistresses dot the walls. Queen Anne's furniture sits in one room, unused, because she never made the trip to Warwick. I guess it's to be expected from a woman who had seventeen miscarriages, was five feet tall, and weighed almost three hundred pounds at the time of her death.

The castle was built in medieval times, around 1200 or so. Its original owner was Earl, Duke of Warwick, who oversaw the death of Joan of Arc. It served as a prison during the sixteenth century until a rich family bought it. They lived there until 1978.

Alexandra and I scampered around, taking pictures, soaking up the atmosphere, climbing ramparts. A Disneyfied version of medieval history, the Kingmaker is a walk-through exhibit partially sponsored by Madame Tussaud's Wax Museum.

Perhaps the most chilling part of the museum was the

torture chamber. Stockades hung from the ceiling. A small iron collar with tiny, spring-loaded spikes sat on a table. And particularly horrifying was the *oubliette*, a shallow chamber in the floor—a deep pothole, really—just big enough to hold a person. A grate sat over it. To explain the torture, I shall resort to etymology: *oubillete* is French for "forgotten".

From there we went to Stratford. On the bus, I had an entertaining discussion with Donald. He's a pretty brilliant philosophy major who is, oddly enough, also an assistant manager at a McDonald's in Grand Rapids. Donald boasts that he's the only person in the world who's attended both Oxford University and Hamburger University, which is what McDonald's calls its training course in Illinois. When people harass him on the job, presuming that he's a moron, he spouts Plato at them. He's afraid of advancing any further in the corporation because "you end up with ketchup running in your veins, man." He's also the last in a long line of Texas Rangers and is obsessed with the phrase "It's a beautiful thing". He says it multiple times a day.

At Stratford, the performance of *The Taming of the Shrew* was fantastic. Josie Lawrence played Kate, the lead. My sister would probably have recognized her from that British improvisation show on Nickelodeon (the name escapes me), where she is a regular.

Some people believe that the Bard's roots in Stratford-upon-Avon is a farce. The William Shakespeare in Stratford was apparently an ignorant farmer who never spelled his name the same way twice. I like a different theory—that Christopher Marlowe faked his own murder to escape the King's agents (who wanted to kill him for having an affair with the king's mistress) and continued to publish his plays from abroad under the name William Shakespeare, an illiterate actor from the sticks. Most probable, though, is the possibility that Shakespeare wasn't one person at all, but a group of writers.

Alastair Lowsley said this morning that the Crown Tavern, William Shakespeare's favorite place in Oxford, was located in the plaza in front of the Covered Market. In fact, if one eats in the upper dining room of Pizzaland, one may be sitting and staring at the same wall Shakespeare stared at while eating his victuals.

The eerie part: Pizzaland was the first restaurant that I dined at the day that I got here.

september 21

. . .

SKIPPED LECTURES TODAY and spent nearly eight hours at the Keble College library, house of books and chamber of frost. When it closed, I filched a book, *Noble Lovers*, to continue studying back in my room for the evening. My rationale: I won't hurt it, nobody will find out, and it's only a rap on my knuckles if someone does. I was wrong on the last count.

Turns out that illegal removal of any library material from the premises results in the library completely denying access to all study-abroad students for an unspecified period of time. Last year, a Keble student was caught eating there, and the enraged librarian closed the library completely for a week and a half—during final exams.

Who is this repressive woman? I've only seen her briefly, enough to know that she walks very briskly. I also know that she complained to Dr. Brown that some student had used a few pieces of paper from the legal pad on her desk while she was away.

september 24

. . .

LUNCHED at the Westgate with Gerda and Alexandra. A real downhome pub meal: vegetable soup, warm bread, roast beef, potatoes, and Yorkshire pudding. Unfortunately it cost almost ten pounds.

We went to the Oxford ice rink after that. Believe me, it is no different from American ice rinks. Heavy black speakers hang menacingly from the ceiling, spitting out savage music by groups with otherwise tranquil names like Oasis and Blur and Tripping Daisy. Young blonde boys careened across the ice like Aryan torpedoes locked in on the break wall.

In order to warm up, I led them out of the arena and down the street to a cozy, carpeted pub I had seen a few days earlier. As we ordered a pot of tea, I began to feel distinctly uncomfortable, as if the other patrons were staring at us. Then a subtle room check and a head count determined that out of the fifteen people there, exactly zero were females. The barkeep was wearing a tight t-shirt and lots of rings. Yes, you may have already guessed it—I accidentally took us into a gay pub. Spare the jokes.

I worked six *straight* hours (pun intended) on my paper that night.

september 26

. . .

I GAINED three new pieces of picture identification today—an International Student ID, a Student Coach Discount, and an Oxford Union Society card. That is three more proofs of my existence.

Dragged myself, limp and confused, to the McDonalds on Cornmarket. We met Gerda's cousin, Johann, and his Japanese friend, Ken. These guys had questionable English skills and were studying at Oxford International Business School, which isn't part of the formal university. They were pretty amused by my antics, and I played right into their stereotype of Americans: loud, funny, obnoxious, etc. I told Johann *holshaften*, which is a foul insult in Swedish. I blamed Ken and his country for the collapse of the automobile industry in Detroit. Sometimes they were laughing at me when I wasn't even trying to be funny. You try to seriously explain the latent irony in Beavis and Butthead without those guys snickering at you. I mean, they didn't even know the word *irony*. I wonder if they know what the word *deportation* means. Not that I, a temporary alien not even registered by the police, have any muscle to threaten them with banishment.

september 27

. . .

THE WEDNESDAY FIELD trip took us to Gloucester Cathedral today.

It's quite gorgeous, a combination of Norman architecture (strong, round, solid, and undecorated) with Gothic (light, airy, upward-sweeping, delicate, perpendicular). I climbed 270 steps to the top of the bell tower. At one point the staircase was exactly as wide as my shoulders and a couple inches higher than me. I wouldn't have been able to grab the handrails even if there were any.

It was a blustery day, and the top of the tower doubly so. Standing on the west side of the catwalk felt like skydiving. We saw clouds rolling in, and when scattered rain started flying sideways across the deck, we scrammed.

On the ground, safely inside the abbey, Edward II is buried, as well as the eldest son of William the Conqueror. I'll say a little more about Edward II in a minute.

I found myself at the Flowers Inn pub (an excellent establishment) and bellied up to a table once again with my constant field trip drinking companion, Dr. Cox-Davies. Gordon and I drank beer, ate kidney pie, and talked.

He said that, back at Oxford, C.S. Lewis' house had

recently been bought by an American ("one of your chaps, with a flair for pizzazz"). The new owner is actively encouraging tour buses to come by, but the house is at the end of a long one-way road and there is no turnabout. So buses have to reverse back to the main road, and many neighbors are quite upset by the disturbances.

Behind Lewis' house lays a big patch of woods that he used as inspiration for the Narnia books. Consequently, they've been renamed Narnia Woods. The funny thing is that Tolkien lived on the other side of these woods and in them also found inspiration for Mirkwood. Cox-Davies revealed that Tolkien occasionally mocked Lewis for including talking animals in his stories. Of course, Cox-Davies is a Welshman, and he said that while Middle Earth isn't explicitly allegorical, you can read a lot of hostility against his own people in the novels. It's rumored that the arrival of the Ringwraiths may have been inspired by an influx of penniless Welshmen into Oxfordshire during the nineteen-thirties.

It reminded me, for some reason, of a story that another student told me recently. A friend of hers at Yale has spotted Harold Bloom, the famous author of *The Western Canon*, one of the world's greatest humanities scholars, in public—and he is slovenly, an absolute pigsty of a human. Another apocryphal story has it that apparently Bloom was sitting on a curb, waiting for a bus, when a passing student threw some change at him and told him to take a bath.

Following lunch, we drove to Barclay Castle. It has been owned by the Barclay family for over 750 years and 24 generations. Pictures of the two sons who are ready to inherit the land, Charles and Henry, elicited sighs and giggles from every woman present, especially Sabina. She's an elitist at heart.

The Barclays' holdings are so extensive that it's said they can hunt from their castle all the way to London on land that they themselves own. That's a long way. Today, most of their money is made from tenant farming. And many castle owners of the late 19th and early 20th centuries married rich American women—daughters of Rockefellers and Carnegies—in order to afford the upkeep of their castles. Indeed, the lord of Blenheim Palace just north of Oxford has reportedly denied his son inheritance because his kid is a drug addict.

There was some good stuff inside of Barclay Castle. Tiny suits of armor, since knights were miniscule. A cup from pre-Saxon England has been on premises continuously since the construction of the castle in 1107. Elizabeth I's bedspread decorated one room. And I learned that it was a Berkeley (same family, different spelling) that Berkeley, California is named for.

Most notoriously, the castle was the site of Edward II's death. His son, Edward III, was on the rise, and his wife, Isabella, was furious as his secret homosexual life. He was imprisoned here above the deep *oubliette*, in the hopes that the fumes from the rotting flesh beneath his feet would eventually kill him. That didn't work, so instead they simply rammed a three-foot-long red-hot iron poker up his ass. Pleasant, civilized times, those were.

England is officially converting to the metric system next month. I hope my country follows soon.

september 30

· · ·

TRIP TO SCOTLAND

3:00 am

It is three o'clock in the morning, and I am sitting in a roadside diner in northern England. I am traveling alone, though I am supposed to meet friends at my destination, Edinburgh. I am tired and feel that I've entered some sort of sleep-deprived alternate dimension. The coach that I am riding is really hot and the woman next to me is from Ireland.

A moment ago, as I slid my cafeteria tray in front of the cashier, she barked something unintelligible at me four times. It didn't sound like English and I didn't know what to do. A man behind me yelled "No" and she grunted and finally rang up my bill. That must be the north country accent that I've heard about. The diner is, ironically, pure Americana, full of neon and advertisements and pinball machines. It is, of course, open around the clock.

Susan, the Irish woman next to me, is a surveyor. Not the land kind. Not the random "Do you have time to fill out this evaluation?" kind. But the kind who estimates how much commercial property is worth. She is nice. We talk about Bono, motorways, and America.

8:00 am

We arrived in Edinburgh two hours ago. Now I am sitting on top of a mountain, still tired as hell. Two hours of fitfully gained sleep on the rubber mat that lines the floor of the aisle of the coach.

Wandering around a strange, barbaric-seeming city at dawn is marvelous. Though scary—my imagination told me that a band of fearsome Celtic warriors was waiting around every corner. An immensely tall, dark, slim column stands in the center of a square. It looks Romanesque, judging from the austere toga-draped figure standing on top.

It seems that the High Street hostel doesn't have room for me. And the bed and breakfast they recommended is full. But a third might have room. I'm waiting until mid-morning to find it and ask.

So here I sit on a mountain in the center of Edinburgh, watching the sun rise over the hills at the edge of the city. My breath is steaming. Also roaming this hilltop are a pack of dogs and one Japanese tourist. He is snapping photos.

Like Zarathustra, I have climbed the mountain, reflected, and am preparing to go back down. Unlike Zarathustra, I believe that God is very much alive. It is my *feet* that are dead.

4:30 pm

Sitting in a second-story pub looking at Edinburgh Castle through the mist and rain.

My hostel, Princes Street Youth Hostel, is actually on Register Street. And High Street hostel is actually on Black-friars Street. Sound like a tourism board conspiracy: keep the under-25 crowd wandering the streets for as long as possible, and maybe they'll drop dead.

Anyhow, the hostel is quite a bohemian place. A large group of kids protesting French nuclear armament is staying there, sporting bullhorns and picket signs that simply read, "*Non*." And they mill through the hallways, exhorting other guests to "Save our environment, save the world, man." This from someone wearing a Rancid shirt.

A very kind woman with short purple hair and a nose ring booked me. There are six beds in my tiny room; I haven't seen any roommates yet. In the dining room, a flotilla of posters, signs, and psychedelic *papier-mâché* creations leave little space for anybody to actually eat.

I haven't encountered anybody who has been completely unintelligible yet, at least not since the woman in the diner last night. Most speak with a soft, lilting brogue. But it *is* gorgeous—both the dialect and the land—and I understand why Sean Connery has "Scotland Forever" tattooed on his wrist.

12:00 am

This may have been the most eventful evening of my life, wracked with great despair, then followed by great hope.

My friends from Oxford never showed. I am here alone.

Fuming and snorting, I grumbled down the street with a tight black storm cloud roiling above my head. After eating at KFC—it was late, don't give me any shit about my Scottish dining experience of choice—I stomped into the Royal Oak tavern.

It's just a wee tiny pub. I ordered a Guinness and sat down to read dejectedly.

"Look a' the busy stoodent," said a woman's voice. "Put down your book."

She and a man were sitting at one of the two other tables.

We edged closer to one another and began talking a little. Or, rather, they talked, and I nodded and pretended to understand their accent. Later in the evening I would presume that they were Irish. I don't know what the hell I was thinking. I've found out that *Since you're from Dublin* is the wrong thing to say to somebody in Scotland.

A pair of University of Edinburgh students sat down between us, and soon all of us were engaged in a conversation about Edgar Allen Poe. He's quite popular here, I guess.

Then the music began. An older woman entered the pub, guitar in hand (all ages mix gracefully in Scottish watering holes, it seems) and began to croon Scottish folk ballads in a beautifully rich brogue. Tales of love, of lust, of hard work and aging wives. One told of the murder of the MacGregor clan—the hanged family in *Braveheart*—and made me *feel* the pain and pride of her people. Others joined in, and the whole room sang the last chorus. Soon men were bursting with limericks all over, and two more guitars walked through the door.

Ann hour later, I excused myself and walked out into the foggy mists. Those people accepted me and made me feel very special, but those experiences have to be capped. It was just brief enough, just delicious enough, to leave me hungry for more.

Scottish folk music, incidentally, isn't too far removed from American country music. They both make use of the same major, minor, and especially minor seventh chords. Lyrically, both sing of courage and hope in the face of pain and hopelessness. I guess the Scottish folk ballad is the basis of our own.

Then I ambled down High Bridge until I heard a different type of music beating down a stairwell. It was a little wooden shack of a nightclub, and the infectious rhythm was courtesy of a five-piece band featuring, among other instruments, a mandolin and a violin. I danced and broiled with happy energy while the lead singer, cute like a pixie, bopped around the small floor like a hyperactive child on a pogo stick. During a slower song she stared at me from behind the mike stand.

I've noticed, in just one day, that Scottish women do fit the famous stereotype. They really are *defiant*. They are stern with their children and they tell it like they see it. Smart mouths, some would call it, or stubborn, but to me it appears to be plain and simple strength.

october 1

. . .

THE TOUR GUIDE at Edinburgh Castle enlightened me today. She was a font of Scottish wit, wisdom, and culture.

For example: She said that since Scots are notoriously cheap, a cannon is fired from the castle at 1 pm every day. Why not noon? Because one shell is cheaper than twelve.

And they have a secret love of pageantry, though they probably wouldn't ever admit it. Witness: the dog cemetery in the castle for Her Highness' royal mutts. Little bitty headstones.

They've also suffered greatly. Oliver Cromwell ransacked Edinburgh looking for the Honours, the Scottish crown jewels, when he ascended to power. When he learned that they had been taken to Dunnottar Castle at Stonehaven, he laid siege to that too. The royal scepter, sword, and crown were carried out of the castle under a woman's skirt and in bundles of flax.

In World War I, over 150,000 Scotsmen gave their lives to God, country, and whiskey (not necessarily in that order). Because Scotland didn't really have too many more people than that, it essentially became a "nation of widows". Perhaps these trials and tribulations are what gave rise to the mournful, melancholy nature of their folk songs. Maybe it goes back even further than that.

Edinburgh Castle is best known for being the birthplace of James VI, also known as James I, king of England and the first of the Stuarts. I stood in the birthing room, and it's not impressive. It's a walk-in closet with a wooden chair. If Bloody Mary, his mother, had kept a well-built midwife, she might have had to give birth through the doorway.

This is the same James who got actively involved in re-editing the Bible to satisfy the demands of the Puritans in his new land. Today we call it the King James Bible. And Jamie Six, as he commonly referred to here, also wrote a treatise in Latin condemning tobacco.

At lunch, I ate *haggis*, the staple of Scottish pub food. It is a curious brown mash, much like Spam or even kibbeh, that immediately becomes much less appetizing when you learn its ingredients—suet, corn, and finely minced sheep lungs and intestines, all boiled together in a sheep stomach, which is removed before serving. *Neeps* (squash or sweet potatoes, I think) and *tatties* (mashed potatoes and turnips) come with it. Seeing the words those words scrawled on a luncheon chalkboard made me question if this truly is the English language or some backwards silkscreen.

I hiked to Newhaven harbor, three miles away, and knelt down and tasted the North Sea. It was disgusting, and I wondered what possessed me to do that. Then I got bored and attempted to take some J Crewish photos along the dock, courtesy of the timer on my camera.

My friends from Oxford finally arrived—Catherine, Carol, and Heather. We drank tea at the High Street hostel and played an inane game with a 50p coin that had its roots in the weighty peek-a-boo line of entertainment.

Then I dragged everybody over to the Royal Oak pub.

They thoroughly enjoyed the live music, though I was disappointed that none of the troubadours knew "Glencoe". And it only took a pint and a half of Guinness before I finally found my Scottish accent, floating there at the bottom of my glass. *Wee*, *lad*, *lass*, and *aye* are all part of my vocabulary now.

october 2

. . .

THERE COMES a time in every person's life when the sublime is revealed. The grandeur of nature, especially vis-à-vis the puny, crumbling architectural efforts of man attests to the fleeting blip that each person is on the cosmic radar screen.

Dunnottar Castle is one of those places that can extract a religious feeling of awe, *mysterium tremendum*, an ineffable and unrelatable experience from everybody. Well, maybe not the squad of English troops that William Wallace burned to death in its chapel in 1297.

At a little after noon, Carol, Heather, and I had rolled into the little hamlet of Stonehaven via a Citylink coach. I spotted a street named Wallace Wynd. A Scotsman's hero, no doubt. And there was another sign that read *Automobiles parking here outwith a sticker will... Outwith*? 'Tis a land of linguistic barbary.

We hiked down a long road and up a gradual incline in pouring rain. I regretted wearing my suede coat, even if I'd bought it from a sketchy vendor wheeling a rack through Gloucester Green in Oxford.

Finally we arrived at the top of the bluffs, and the view

was astounding. The tiny village lay at our feet, and the North Sea spread all around, looking cold and fearsome and not unlike the Great Lakes back home.

To describe each breathtaking view would fill this slim journal. Suffice to say that for the next mile we wandered down a little-used sheep path that hugged the edge of the steep bluffs, only three feet wide, the ocean crashing loudly against the cliff below us. We encountered three herds of sheep (dumb, woolly brutes) and only three other people.

Then Dunnottar Castle appeared out of the fog, and it took my breath away. A little background first. There has probably been some sort of fortress or garrison on this site since 631. It guarded the Royal Honours from Cromwellian thugs in 1651. And more recently, Mel Gibson's version of *Hamlet* was filmed there.

It's reached by walking down a low, narrow isthmus. We did so quickly, and for the next hour I regressed to my child-hood, clambering and scampering and capering around the grounds. Lots of dank, musty, decrepit rooms and storehouses and stairs to explore. We scared a flock of pigeons—excuse me, *flying rats*—when we crept into the castle prison. And, of course, we peered through every little rectangular aperture afforded by the medieval construction at the whitecapped oceanic vista below us.

I had to leave early to catch a coach to Aberdeen to get to Perth to … forget it. It's too complicated to waste space on. What ultimately transpired was that I hiked down a small two-lane road through the bright Scottish countryside, cows leering at me through barbed wire fence, the North Sea shining bright and blue to my right.

On the coach, a very drunk man sat behind me. He was in poor shape. He moved with that excruciating slowness that only chronic drunks can have. I watched him in the reflection of the window.

Presently he leaned forward and in a raspy voice asked, "Would … you have a … light?"

I looked at the cigarette dangling from his lip. "No," I said, "I don't carry lighters. Sorry."

He seemed genuinely perplexed by this. A minute later, his booze-addled brain decided to rewind the tape.

"Do … you … have … a … light?"

"No sir," I replied. "I have no fire of any kind, match-books, lighters, or otherwise."

He sat back, mumbling, and started fishing around in his pockets. He pulled out a lighter and lit his cigarette. The smoke wafted up and down the length of the coach.

Then an enormous voice bellowed from the front of the bus: "NO SMOOKIN' ON THE COOCH!"

It was the driver, his fierce eyes staring at him in the rearview mirror. The man blinked stupidly, then shrugged and extinguished his cigarette in the ashtray. But he was so drunk that he didn't realize that he'd forgotten to pull the ashtray down, and plunged the orange glowing tip of the cigarette onto his own thigh.

"Ow," he said.

When I got off the bus an hour later, he was passed out, head hanging between his knees.

october 3

. . .

THE OVERNIGHT COACH pulled into Oxford's Gloucester Green at 8:45 this morning. I tried to shake the sleep out of my eyes. It was going to be a day filled with political rhetoric.

First was Tony Blair, head of the Labour Party, speaking at a conference on BBC2. I watched the speech on television in the common room and analyzed it from an oratorical point of view. He was emotional, impassioned, and intelligent. And he exhibited that wry English sense of humor. He's something of a socialist and his speech reaffirmed that tradition.

In the evening, I went to the Oxford Union to listen to a speech, live and in person, by former U.S. vice-president Dan Quayle. Of course, he's a national punchline for his massacre of the English language, but he spoke with almost no blunders, except for a reference to America as "this country". He also insisted on recycling great quotations of the past, though he left the United Negro College Fund well enough alone.

What was more disheartening, actually, was his lack of improvisation. He fudged more questions than he answered, pleading "I don't want to get into that". At other times he rehashed common knowledge to avoid offering a substantive answer.

There was the inevitable spud comment. "Mr. Quayle," said one student, raising his hand during the question-and-answer session, "I'm having an essay crisis. I'm writing a paper on eighteenth-century crop rotation, and I need to know how to spell the word *potato*."

To me, the funniest moment of the night was hearing a student from Taiwan bow, then address him as "Your Excellency".

After the talk ended, I battled my way up through the crowd to the former vice president. It was my right to meet him, as one of maybe four Americans in the room. I shook Quayle's hand and we looked each other in the eye. Knowing full well his anger with the Beltway media establishment, I asked, "Mr. Quayle, why on earth would you want to go *back* to Washington?" He had mentioned running for national office again in his speech.

He laughed. As he began to drift past me, in a dreamlike tone he said, "To solve all the problems."

Such heroic aspirations! Such selfless abasement for the commonweal! A martyr to the General Will! If only we had more mediocre sons of wealthy men to charge into Washington, holding gleaming cellular phones and faxing simplistic ideas about downsizing government!

Some low wattage there.

october 5

. . .

TODAY I WALKED TO THE FRESHERS' Fair, the one day every year that all of Oxford University's shady clubs, associations, and societies slither into the sunlight and try to recruit new members. Everything is on offer: a Tiddlywinks Club, the Dr. Who Society, the C.S. Lewis Association, Hangliders' Club, the Christ Church Choristry, and the Gay and Lesbian Society, whose representatives wondered rather loudly about my sexual orientation as I walked past.

I got a little testy with the Society of Nonconformity (which is an oxymoron, if you think about it).

"There's nothing more bourgeois than trying not to look bourgeois," I said.

Behind the table, the skinny guy with the mohawk started to glower at me. "You can fill out our survey if you'd like."

"Yes, I *would* like," I said. I took the clipboard and began to circle every answer choice on his multiple-choice non-conformist survey.

"You can't do that," he said.

"Why not?" I answered.

He thought about it, but evidently couldn't think of a

reply. Just as he was really starting to get his nosering in a knot, I went ahead and joined his silly group.

Then Gerda and Alexandra and I visited the Union, for it was having another event. Same day, different fair. What I found was enough free swag to ... well, satisfy an American. Pizza, chocolate, ice cream, even Mad Dog 20/20 shots—everything flowed plentifully.

We glided away from the Mad Dog table and down to the Cellar Bar in the Union. That's when my two companions hatched their devious scheme. Drink after drink after drink found their way into my hand, and an hour later I stumbled out into the warm, sunny afternoon. I was totally stewed. At five o'clock I tripped my way into my Chaucer lecture. It was the first time I've ever gone to class drunk. I don't think Alastair noticed, or if he did, he probably approved.

october 6

· · ·

WE LIVE in an age where the only absolute is vodka.

october 7

. . .

THE DRINKING BEGAN at four-thirty in the afternoon. Sitting on the floor of Kevin's room, Gerda and others forced strange, alien concoctions down my throat. They contained hot coffee, whipped cream, and Frangelico.

Then we headed to the Kings' Arms for dinner. I talked with Jennifer, another student from my home university. She was studying abroad in Leuven and had come across the English Channel to spend a couple of days with her friend Catherine. Belgium hasn't changed her, not one bit. She's uncomfortable in her own skin and didn't even acknowledge Alexandra when she entered the room. A waste of flesh. Sorry, but it's how I feel.

That night, Alexandra and I talked Big Talk at the Union bar. Love, life, the human condition, teleology, Page Three girls—you name it. Then we scooted to the Chequers pub, a huge party scene in a historic alley.

We followed that with two hours of hardcore dancing at the Dolly. High points included Shaggy's "Boombastic" and Snoop Dogg—I grooved hard to that one. Low points included Bon Jovi and synthesized eurocrap, as well as the alternately passed-out-then-suddenly violent guy dancing next to me.

october 8

. . .

TODAY I TOOK a hike inside Christ Church college. A bowler-hatted guard gave me an attitude until I flashed the Bodleian ID. Then he backed off. Typical reaction when tough guys see a library card, I know.

It was quite warm. The Tom Quad is enormous and has that damn Jupiter fountain in the middle. The Church itself was cute. A memorial to St. Frideswide lay in a side chapel.

The Great Hall is something else entirely. It looks much like Keble Dining Hall, except for the portraits of its famous graduates that line the walls. It's like a roll call of Western Civ. There was John Locke, Charles Boyle, John Randolph, and Charles Dodgson, known better as Lewis Carroll. And so many Williams—William Pitt, William Penn, William Gladstone, just to name a few. A huge portrait of Henry VIII hangs at one end, with the very famous one of Queen Elizabeth I next to him.

Then I hiked down to the Thames to watch the first day of rowing practice. Spandex-clad girls trotted around the docks like mermaids coming to the surface.

october 10

· · ·

AT THE OXFORD UNION this afternoon, I listened to Andrew Sullivan, editor of *The New Republic* and author of *Virtually Normal*. He was the Oxford Union president in 1983.

A bit disappointing. I had expected a famous editor and writer and bomb thrower to be more … *interesting*.

We met not in the main hall, but in the Old Library, so it was very crowded. I raised my hand and asked a question. "Mr. Sullivan, what has been the reaction from the political left to the fifth chapter of your book, especially in light of your editorship?"

He smirked, and then managed to bore me for the next ten minutes with a torturously long answer. I gathered only this: public institutions must change and set new standards for private citizenry to follow. Discuss.

october 11

. . .

MY FIRST OFFICIAL TUTORIAL.

For four weeks, we study-abroad student have been listening to lectures *en masse*. That was because we arrived so early, a full month before school technically began. Now that the official Michelmas term has started, and all the British students have arrived, the traditional method of education has truly begun.

My first tutor is a professor named Amanda Wentworth. I'm reading Shakespeare with her, approximately twenty plays in ten weeks, with a five-page essay to be written on each. That's a hundred pages of literary analysis. There is also another student, Ryan.

Amanda is a very sharp woman, and our first session was a bit tough. She has a brisk, *and-quickly-what-is-your-name* type of attitude that made me feel like a bit of a commodity. Bring the students in, get them well-read, send them along.

We convened in her office, which is nothing more than a rented bedroom in a rowhouse on Beaumont Street. Ryan and I sat on the edge of the spare mattress, sitting uncomfortably erect. She curled up in an overstuffed blue Victorian chair. A small card table was at her knees, holding her mug of tea. She didn't offer us any. She rubbed cream into her hands while we took turns reading our papers out loud.

Mine was on the loss of freewill in *MacBeth*. At times Dr. Wentworth nodded encouragingly. At other times, she shook her head side-to-side, harrumphed, made a note, or gave other nonverbal clues as to the quality of my thoughts. When I finished, she asked very precise questions about the essay. I was able to fend them off. At no time did she physically touch the paper, or even ask to read anything. Everything is spoken. At no time did she offer a grade, either. I get the sense that my final mark will be granted, shall we say, *holistically*, so I'm being sure to dress well for the sessions.

Still, I like her, and I'm up for the challenge of a pair of Shakies a week. There are videotapes of all thirty-two plays available at the library, which should help. I can't think of a better place to finally dive into his work.

october 12

. . .

THIS WAS the evening of my first formal debate at the Oxford Union Society.

Let me clarify. It wasn't *my* debate. I didn't participate. I just watched it.

The Debating Hall is a large room with several rows of padded benches facing each other. This is for the audience. In between lay the debating stand, and a dais with three chairs overlooks everything. On the whole it looks a lot like the set of Family Feud.

The pageantry of the pre-debate proceedings was impressive. Officers sat on the dais in dinner tuxedoes. The secretary read the minutes from the last meeting out of a large book bound in red velvet. The librarian delivered his list of recommended reading for the week, which I didn't quite understand, and then made fun of the president's penis. The president then stood up, made fun of his own penis ("If any honorable member of this Union—other than my own..."), and introduced the speakers.

The topic was pornography. On the pro-side sat three people: 1) P.J. Taylor, the goofy ex-editor of the *Cherwell*, 2) a contributing editor of *Penthouse*, and 3) Debee Ashby, ex-Penthouse Pet of the Year. On the anti-side sat a stern, retributive, stocky woman. She saw no humor in anything, only pain. At one point during the proceedings, she pointed her finger at a libertarian student in the middle of his question and shouted, "Lies, lies—*all lies!*" Another student, an American named Jessica, was given the floor and made some very good points. Lastly, somebody named Lord Longford, chair of something called the Longford Commission on Pornography, was given the floor. He also had some wise insights, even though he looked like he hadn't had sex since the Churchill administration.

I heard very good evidence from both sides of the pornography debate; so much, in fact, that I still can't make up my mind about which is the correct path for society to follow. F. Scott Fitzgerald said that the test of a first-rate intelligence is the ability to hold two opposing viewpoints at the same time and still retain the ability to function.

There are no easy answers.

october 13

. . .

I READ *HENRY IV, Part 2* from cover to cover while sitting in the Old Library at the Union. The Old Library is a massive, domed oaken room lined with ancient books and filled with cushy leather chairs. It feels like it was plucked out of a Hollywood set designer's imagination, but it's as real as anything.

At midnight, in the empty common room of my building, I turned on the VHS player and slid in a Tori Amos video, *Little Earthquakes*, that I had rented at the library hours earlier. Within minutes, nearly every woman within earshot had been drawn to the screen like moths to a flame, pulled in by some ancient current of shared femininity. I heard soft gasps and little chokes behind me as Tori's face floated angelically on the screen.

october 15

· · ·

A DAY TRIP that epitomizes the Oxford experience. Alexandra and I hopped on a bus to Blenheim Palace in nearby Woodstock.

We walked through an enormous gate onto the sprawling estate. There are 2500 acres of rolling meadows, grassy embankments, lawns, odd gardens designed by Capability Brown, and a scenic river that may or may not have been the Thames. I never found out.

The palace itself is very well-preserved, probably because it is relatively new. Winston Churchill was born and died there, though he spent all his years in between elsewhere. Oriental collectors' china and seventeenth-century Flemish tapestries fill what feels like the hundreds of rooms inside. The owners of the castle had more money than they knew what to do with, and clearly they wanted to Make A Statement of some sort.

However, we spent most of our time outdoors. I climbed an old hollow oak on the riverbank that brought to mind Berenstein's Spooky Old Tree. We capered madly on the wide lawns and snapped photos of the hilariously phallic trees.

When that grew tiresome, we jumped on the mini-railroad

that rumbled through the dappled sheep pastures and found our way to the Pleasure Gardens. The name conjures up the image of a Teutonic woman in skintight leather garb and stiletto heels, using a riding crop to whip an old boxer-shorted British gentlemen in the petunia.

No, it was more of a children's playground, but a really good one. A putting green, bouncy castles, a hedge maze, and an overgrown chess board all amused us for a while.

Walking back to the palace, we cut through herds of sheep, which ambled away across the grass as we approached. Since everyone wants what they can't have, my goal became clear: I want to catch a sheep. Just one.

When we got back to the large gate we had originally entered through, we found that it had closed. We'd missed closing time by ten minutes, and in England, customer service isn't exactly high on the list of national priorities.

We were locked in.

I stood there, dumbfounded, staring at the gate. It was twenty feet high and had speared points. We weren't getting over that thing. A high stone wall ran in either direction. We could hear the traffic rushing along the busy street on the other side.

Panicking and laughing at the same time, Alexandra and I ran through backyards, over short fences, and through horse pastures in search of a point where we could possibly get over the wall. We found it, climbed a small fence, hoisted ourselves over the top, and dropped fifteen feet down to the grass on the other side. At that exact moment, the bus back to Oxford pulled up and opened its doors. We nonchalantly strolled onto the bus. It couldn't have been timed better.

At the Union that night, I attended a debating workshop for freshers. For some reason, I qualify as one of them, even though I'm a junior back in the U.S. A highly excitable chap operated the workshop. His head flicked from side to side—all his features and actions and behaviors look like they are in fast forward. God help him. The ulcer ward at Oxford General has probably already granted him "most favored patient" status.

He organized a mock debate for us newbies upon the resolution: *This house calls for a return to Thatcherism*. Thankfully I didn't have to speak. All that lights up in my mind when Maggie is mentioned is her great chumminess with Ronald Reagan, and talking about friendship between sovereigns for three minutes probably wouldn't have cut it.

october 17

· · ·

LONDON

The day of all days. Anthony, my friend from our home college, arrived from Rome, where he is studying abroad. With him was his girlfriend, Christina—a charming, intelligent Noo Yawker.

Our activities were varied and aimless. We hung out like laundry in St. James Park, looking at ducks, talking big talk. We goofed through Westminster Abbey. We saw Big Ben. Our friend Sabina failed to meet us at the appointed time, so we plowed on without her.

Anthony has become more interesting in the past six months. No longer is the politician/lawyer mold inarguably in his future. He's contemplating, among other things, social work and psychiatry.

"Italy is wonderful," he told me, "but it's made me more of a patriot. I am not an Italian. I am not an Italian-American. I am an *American*."

I commented that perhaps black Americans needed a

couple of months in Mogadishu to persuade them to drop the "African" word from their monikers. He agreed.

In Rome, he said, the Tiber River is so filthy that anyone who falls in must by law be rushed to a hospital and decontaminated. And he said that women in Rome are yelled and screamed at by men everywhere. The result is that they won't look at men on the street. Any man who wants to speak to a woman formally must be introduced first.

He also said that the Rome subway only has two lines. All plans for other lines were abandoned after workers ran into too many buried ancient ruins beneath the streets of the city.

Italy has seen 54 prime ministers since World War II. That's one every nine months. They still can't seem to agree on anything. They're not a country, not really, just a loose conglomeration of city-states.

As night fell and the neon blinked on, we found our way into SoHo. The Chinatown section is pulsing, throbbing, vibrant. We stopped at a restaurant named Fok Hoo Inn. Over a plate of duck, it occurred to me that Chinatown, by itself, is a good argument for imperialism. I told Anthony that Britain would never have benefitted from this culture had they not bluntly carved out spheres of influence in China in the nineteenth century. Anthony said that I was sounding like P.J. O'Rourke.

Cruising through the red-light sex district of Soho was interesting. Neither of us, nor his girlfriend, had really seen that kind of stuff before. I'm not sure I want to see it again.

We investigated bookshops. We blatantly used a Pizza Hut for its bathroom. We enjoyed two drinks at the Long Island Iced Tea cocktail club, which is a discotheque with the type of loud *woompa-woompa* buzzsaw dance music that forces over-pronounced lip movement. Later, at Ed's, a Johnny Rockets ripoff, a waiter treated us with little less than outright hostility. I was disappointed. Part of me assumed that everybody loves Americans, at least for ten minutes or so. We made like a banana and left.

The London subway is like the mythical Greek labyrinth in which Theseus battled the Minotaur. I almost wanted to trail a thread behind me. Washington D.C.'s Metro system looks like it was designed by Fisher Price by comparison.

At Buckingham Palace, Anthony struggled to take a picture of "those guys with the big fuzzy black hats". I was pretty bored. The Queen was scheduled to arrive at twelve-thirty, but we didn't want to wait around to get a glimpse of her. She's only a titular head of state anyhow. It's sort of like mulling around Massachusetts Avenue waiting for Dan Quayle's motorcade to pass by. I'm sure my new close personal friend understands that there's no offense meant.

The Queen is apparently travelling with the king of Finland. Anthony and I are two well-educated, politically-minded college students, but we couldn't recall a single fact about Finland, much less its royal office.

october 20

. . .

THERE ARE PROMISING days in everybody's lives that
turn out to be lemons, disappointing, overly hyped. There are
also very low-key day that gear up beneath your feet and
behind your back, exploding into big shimmering parades
with confetti and wonder and magic. Today was the second
type.

Sabina woke me up at ten o'clock in the morning. I bathed
quickly and was ready forty-five minutes later. We walked to
Gloucester Green, where we met Narek, a quiet, black-eyed
Armenian whose quiet demeanor sheaths a very active mind.
He's American too. We boarded a coach and rode the two
hours into London.

Our destination was the Barbican, London's home of the
Royal Shakespeare Company. We'd heard stories of students
who were able to procure tickets to their performances, same
day, at great discount. This is important because a ticket to
one of these shows normally costs fifty pounds or more, and
none of us have much money.

We arrived at the theater in the early afternoon and
headed directly to the box office. To our wonderment, the
clerk immediately sold us three tickets for that evening's

performance of *A Midsummer Night's Dream*. The cost: Six pounds each. We performed jigs of exultation.

Excited, we groped our way down into a cavernous London pub called the Vaults. It was filled with pinstripey members of the London business sector—the Fleet Street set, I guess. We ate heartily and drank beer, though not too much. We dared not the risk of being walled alive in our booth the way the drunken Fortunato was in another set of vaults.

In the afternoon, we found the excavation site of the original Globe Theater. It's just southeast of the south end of the Southwark Bridge. (That's a lot of souths.) Here's the sad part: it doubles as a car park. Peugeots sit at the very lip of the pit. It's ironic. The foundations of the most theater of the greatest playwright to ever use the English language are, after four hundred years, in danger of destruction not by fire, flood, or erosion... but by falling Volvos.

The security guard who let us into the car park seemed thoroughly nonplussed by the immense historical significance of the site he was supposed to be guarding. "I's jus' a bloody 'ole inna ground," he said.

The new Shakespeare Globe Museum Centre is under construction, and it's going to be good stuff. An exact replica of the Globe, down to wooden pegs and all, will be opened in June. (This one, however, has fire exits, sprinklers, and a lighting crew.) It is still outdoors; performances are going to be held in the afternoons only, but finances may dictate otherwise.

Walking across the city, we passed by many rows of windows looking into huge rooms of office workers, mostly spry young men in crisp yellow, white, and blue starched shirts. Most of the faces were turned looking at me—or, more precisely, at Sabina walking alongside me. She's a tall blonde and was dressed very stunningly. I've never seen her less than beautiful.

St. Paul's Cathedral was our next destination, and it was

incredible. I thought that seeing the basilica in D.C., not to mention all these weeks of touring other cathedrals, had made my appreciation of old religious buildings as calloused as my mother's feet. Not so. Christopher Wren's final master-piece was sublime, especially as it towered into the overcast sky of a charcoal gray dusk. I tried to get close to the altar, but a stern woman put her hand into my face and enunciated the word "No" very clearly. I poured wave upon wave of charm, yet the hand remained. Damn Anglican.

We wandered around the business district for a while, exploring the dark alleys and oaken facades described in the Sherlock Holmes stories.

Finally we found our seats at the Barbican for the produc-tion, and it was astounding—magical, mystical, invigorating, sparkling, you name it. Of course, it would take a real bone-head of a director to mess up such a perfect script. ("I've got a radical new interpretation of Dream, Bob—*funeral dirges*! Puck sits weeping in a corner! Fairies draped in black hover around a coffin! The world will love it!")

In my short life thus far, this was the first Shakespeare play that has the stamp of genius marked upon it. The final benediction, delivered by Puck, had us gasping, so crystalline was the language and flawless the delivery. The play hasn't been described as Mozartian for nothing.

However, the subway ride back to Victoria Station was a disaster. The British don't believe in labeling their trains, even if two or more lines run on the same track. Then we encoun-tered a lunatic at Paddington Station. He stood authorita-tively with piercing eyes and an evilly hunched back, a grimy guitar slung around his shoulder on a string. He talked to himself *at us*, if you get my meaning. Then he turned to a bill-board advertising a retro-doowop outfitted entertainer named Gary Glitter.

The lunatic began stabbing at the poster with his index finger. "You ... you're just a prop. Jimi Hendrix—who was that? Eric Clapton is a set up. He's a fool. Homosexuality is for the toilets. No, I'm *not* talking about anything! I've been having this conversation since 1978!"

Rage, rage, at the dying of the light … inside his skull. We edged further down the platform and waited for the subway car to take us home.

october 22

. . .

LOTS OF STUDYING TODAY. I helped Adam, the no-hands man, eat a chicken drumstick. When you don't have any hands, that's a difficult task. I took the meat off the bones for him.

Then I finally asked him the question that had been bothering me for almost two months. The one that he surely is sick of answering.

It was a long answer, but I'll summarize here. Frat party at his home university. Too much liquor. Pipe bomb prank.

Boom.

He said he woke up two days later, remembering nothing of the accident.

Now he's a man driven. Or, I should say, a man biking. After the spring term ends, he is determined to ride his bicycle across Wales, alone, for two months next spring. It's a hot-rod mountain bike, imported here from the States, and "specially customized for a no-hands man". He loves calling himself that.

october 26

. . .

I DELIVERED two speeches in a single day.

The first was my regular weekly oratory, this time on the nature of the "special relationship" between the U.S. and the U.K. Alastair was pleased by my voice modulation, hand movements, rhetoric.

The second was to my Chaucer seminar group. It was on *fabliau*, or bawdy stories in medieval France. The class was particularly fond of my phrase, "He was then beaten like a gong." Alastair put his head between his knees and howled with laughter. I was taken aback. It was amusing, sure, but not meant to evoke rip-roaring, knee-slapping, pig-snorting great guffaws of laughter. I *know* I'm not that funny, and I stole it from Hunter S. Thompson anyways.

After it was all over, I ran back to my room and ripped open a bottle of red wine. In the kitchen, a friend named Makenna and I tried to muddle our way through cooking a stir fry. The more we drank, the more we flung peapods and chicken all over the counter. The flecks of boiling vegetable oil that landed on my arm didn't hurt after a while. Things got even worse when Donald poked his head into the kitchen, sussed out our state, and easily persuaded us to dump

Worcestershire sauce and chili powder into our concoction. I won't forgive him for taking advantage of drunk people like that.

We headed out with another girl named Rachel to the Wheatsheaf, where Makenna regaled us with stories of her drug use, her trip to Amsterdam, her parents' newfound love of the religious right, and so on.

After the pub booted us out at closing time, we tripped our way across town, to the flat where Bill Clinton lived when he was a Rhodes Scholar. I should explain my connection to this.

———

I met President Clinton earlier this year. It was Young Journalists' Day at the White House, and I won a lottery among the editorial staff of my school newspaper for one of the two coveted tickets. It was kind of like Charlie Bucket going to the Willy Wonka factory.

Truth be told, though, I hadn't known that I would be meeting the president. I just thought I would just be sitting through some boring speeches by bureaucrats.

It was much more than that. I sat in the front row for a talk by George Stephanopolous, a communications director (I think) and a former Rhodes Scholar himself. Secretary of Labor Robert Reich delivered a great speech and conducted an even better question-and-answer session. His sense of humor was fantastic.

In the afternoon, all three hundred of us filed into the East Room and sat down. I elbowed aside a skinny kid from Yale so that I could sit in the front row. To my surprise, the next speaker was not another bureaucrat, but the actual leader of the free world, right there, in the flesh, not more than fifteen feet in front of me. The pride of Arkansas. It was broadcast on CSPAN.

When he finished, a staffer announced that he wanted to meet each of us personally. After thirty minutes' wait in the receiving line, my stomach in agony from having skipped breakfast and lunch, President Clinton finally turned towards me and grapsed my hand.

"Mister President," I said, a little shakily, "I'm going to follow in your footsteps and study at Oxford University this fall."

(I'm not following in his footsteps at all, but I wanted to flatter him.)

President Clinton seemed surprised. "That's great. I remember my college days there with great fondness. I even visited a couple years ago, but, you know, it's not the same when you're president."

My laugh came out forced because I was so nervous. "*Hahahahahahahahaha.*"

He never let go of my hand the whole time. It's a habit that lots of politicians have, a way to control.

"What college at Oxford did you go to, Mister President?" I said.

"Olif," he said.

I filed that name away. After another fumbling attempt at conversation, he finally released my hand, and turned to the next person in line. I stumbled off, and a few weeks later, my parents received the photos in the mail from the White House. My extended family has started calling me Forrest Gump, for the way that he stumbles into famous people.

———

All that was in April, and I remembered *Olif College* all through the summer. When I arrived here, I began to search for it. I asked everybody in the city about a college named Olif, but nobody had heard of it. I scanned lists of the thirty-eight colleges at Oxford University. It was nowhere to be found.

Stumped, I finally did a little bit of actual research, and I found that as a Rhodes Scholar at Oxford, President Bill Clinton had attended *University* College, and that the name is often shortened to Univ. Then it hit me. The president had said the word *Univ*, but I had been so nervous that my ear had heard *Olif*. I've spent over a month looking for a college that didn't even exist.

In the course of the research, though, I found his old Oxford address: 46 Leckford Road. He lived there for two years, and his flatmates said that he used to eat bacon right out of the pan at the stove. Why bother with a plate, I guess.

I've walked by the house a few times. It's nothing special, but it makes me feel a tiny personal connection to my ten seconds with the most powerful person in the world.

october 27

. . .

O, the horror! Agony of agonies! God, why have you forsaken me?

When you haven't had to endure any discomfort in your life, a backache is like that jolt that comes when you bite down on aluminum foil.

It started in the bathtub. I was laying there in the water when all the muscles in my back suddenly seized up. The pain was like nothing I've ever experienced, and I somehow pulled myself to my feet without screaming.

I lurched down the hallway like Quasimodo. It became even worse when I got to my room. At my sink, a spasm so severe doubled me over so that my head was crammed beneath the faucet. I lay down on the floor, gasping. I don't remember who, but somebody dropped a bottle of ibuprofen into my hand. With one hand, I somehow twisted off the childproof cap, placed two tablets on my tongue, and dragged myself up to the sink again for water.

Later, I limped down the hall to see Rosie Robertson, the Registrar with the Ramrod up her Rear, for help. She told me not to go to the doctor. She told me she had no heating pad.

She told me to not come any closer, please, she has a terrible cold.

No love lost there.

I spent the night laying on a towel of ice cubes in my room, the wedges of cold digging into my back. I feel old. This is the sort of stupid accident that elderly people get when they walk too quickly down the stairs or open a refrigerator door without stretching first.

october 29

· · ·

ANOTHER DAY TRIP. Today's destination: Canterbury.

At seven-thirty am—the earliest I've woken up so far—Josh and I headed out the door. A coach to London, then a local train to Canterbury. Four hours of travelling with no food. My head was swimming with dizziness and hallucinations began. I dreamed that the Beatles were getting back together. I began to think that I actually liked their music. I imagined that Newt Gingrich had a heart.

Josh and I arrived at the town and found the perfect Sunday morning brunch nook. It was a warm, small, cedar-paneled restaurant called Flap-Jacques—"The best of English and French cuisine". They piped in Vivaldi and Rachmaninov through the speakers. Sunday papers sat on a small table near the door. I ate strawberry crepes and a spinach omelette. Soon a man sat down at a piano and began tinkling out some jazz chords. We felt totally content.

The Canterbury Cathedral is gorgeous, especially the nave. But haven't I written the same thing about all the other cathedrals? I guess what sets this one apart is the fact that Thomas Becket was murdered there, on the altar, by three knights who took King Henry II's grumbling a little bit too literally: *Will no one rid me of this meddlesome priest?*

We found a charming park along the river that flows through the town. I kicked around a soccer ball with some pubescent kid who apparently didn't know a word of English. It didn't matter. We connected on an athletic level.

october 31

· · ·

THIS WAS my very first Halloween without any carved pumpkins. Such are the costs of study-abroad programs.

But we did have a stompin' little dance in the Common Room. A bowl of punch, some wine, Donald acting as DJ—it was a beautiful thing.

Sabina put a black wig on and looked absolutely frightful. Sam's hair was out of control, and in his toga he looked like the Bozo Messiah. Julia made a very convincing Janis Joplin. Dennis went as a grotesque, bearded Hester Prynne from *The Scarlet Letter*. Narek went as Dennis, which was hilarious. I went as nothing because I procrastinated finding a costume for too long. And Dr. Brown went as himself, an Oxford don. You haven't lived until you've seen an elderly, conservative professor dancing alone to the Village People.

The highlight of the evening, however, was reading the bizarre note that Mrs. Finlay had given to Dr. Brown. He'd accidentally left it sitting on a table, and we all took turns reading and giggling at it. It was a set of instructions concerning the party, mixed with philosophical reflections on the nature of revelry. A sample: "Control the drink, and end it early, before all their illusions turn into reality." She also

apparently hates loud music, which makes no sense, since she's deaf.

Yes indeed, Mrs. Finlay is quite a case study. She told Sabina that to properly sculpt a bird she needed to "run outside and behave like one". It's said that she assigns room-mates using astrology. Richard Green told me that they once finished off a bottle of gin together, which Mrs. Finlay promptly threw over her shoulder, shattering it against the wall.

november 2

. . .

SOMETIMES MY ORATORY tutorial is less like a proper class and more like an hour of creative expression.

This was legal week, and Alastair told me to create a case to be tried in court. He was judge, the Right Honorable Alastair Lowsley.

So I dreamed up a ludicrous case: attempted spermicide. I recruited Shariq to play the defending barrister, Dennis to play the defendant, and Narek to play a witness. I filled the case with imaginative evidence and told everybody to improvise.

Boy, did they ever. Threw me more than a couple of curveballs. Dennis picked his nose during his testimony. He explained that on the night of the incident he was in Brussels watching a movie with Princess Fergie. Shariq, meanwhile, was splendid as a lawyer. He took it very seriously. He wants to teach law someday, and it shows.

Alastair showed that classic British sense of absurd humor. He made witnesses place their hands on a Shakespeare folio when they were sworn in. He summarized with hilarity. He overruled my objections somewhat harshly (though with a wink). And he cheered and applauded, like a good neutral judge, when our jury convicted Dennis on all counts of aggravated spermicide.

november 3

. . .

WALES

Rose at six o'clock am and was sitting on a train by seven o'clock with Narek. We made it almost all the way to Caerphilly before our ticket was checked.

We found Caerphilly Castle rather quickly, since it's the centerpiece of the town. Built in 1285, it was the first castle to utilize a series of concentric circles to ward off attack: wall, moat, wall, moat, wall. We had the entire site to ourselves because we arrived so early.

Don't get the impression that it's been seriously restored. It hasn't. In fact, it's in ruins. One whole tower has cracked in half and is leaning crazily ten degrees to the east. I think I like it better that way. Like Glastonbury, seeing Nature reclaim her own is much more spectacular than the arrogant little attempts of man to retain his little dominion.

Walking down a street, we saw a sign saying "Bookstore and Tea Room – Fresh Homemade Cakes – Come In!" It turned out to be the lobby of a church. Folding tables and paper cups were the primary décor. Christian books with titles like Finding God sat on a shelf. A fat old woman waddled around trying to serve the five people there.

We sat down with a man who had a mechanical device taped to his throat. When he pressed its button and spoke, his voice came out like a synthesized piece of robotics. He sounded like a talking electric shaver, if electric shavers could talk.

He asked me about my hometown, then we chatted about the Wye Valley. He asked me if I had ever gone to church. When I said yes, he proudly said that this was a Church of Nonconformity that I was sitting in. Celtic people seem to pride themselves on that.

By and by, we made our way to Tintern, a small village nestled in the hills of the Wye Valley. It is dominated by colossal ruins of Tintern Abbey, an eleventh-century Cistercian abbey that was for many years the richest in Britain. It was dissolved with all the other monasteries by Henry VIII in 1536. In literary circles, it's known mostly for the famous poem that Wordsworth wrote about it in the late 1700s.

Those monks had it good. They grew plenty of food, had a huge cathedral, and enjoyed private quarters bigger than any dorm I've ever lived in. They entertained all kinds of visitors and housed lay brothers. One wonders how "monkish" they really were. I bet it was more of an exclusive club filled with beer and illegitimate children.

The country really is gorgeous here, the ruins of the abbey tucked inside this colorful valley. But, to tell the truth, it looks a lot like upstate New York or any other part of the northern Appalachians. Turner painted Tintern; Cole painted Hudson Valley. All those Romantics were on the same vibe.

Having met Catherine and Evelyn at the abbey, we decided to walk the five miles back to Chepstow. Unfortunately, there was no river walk, as we had expected. We were forced to walk on the edge of the shoulderless road. Things became pretty hairy in the curvy mountains. Then the sun went down, and we were walking in pitch black.

At about five-thirty we passed an old farmhouse with—there *is* a God—a whole yard of buses next to it. Four men were working on one of them, and they agreed to give us a ride back to Chepstow in a minute. We loaded onto a bright blue bus and soon one of the guys came and started it up. We clattered onto the main road and passed over the moonlit Welsh countryside.

"Ye know ye're on the dribble boos," our driver said.

We all looked at each other, unsure what he meant.

I cleared my throat. "Why do you call it the *dribble bus,* sir?"

"It carries handicapped kids," he replied.

———

Back in town, we found a delightful pub called the Beaumont. I had one of the warmest, kindest dinners of my life: Welsh rarebit, buttered mushrooms, and a pint of beer. We talked about coursework, feminism, and Christianity until the others had to catch their train back home to Oxford.

I was officially alone in Wales. Three days of glorious freedom to explore. I found my way to my bed and breakfast. Eileen, the proprietor, sat me down in her enormous kitchen and served me some hot tea and began talking. She is a retired opera singer who now runs this two-hundred-year-old mansion for some extra money. She'd travelled all around the world. The only place that she felt distinctly uncomfortable, she said, was Detroit.

Then the only other person in the mansion, a boarder, lurched into the kitchen. He was totally plastered.

"I'm not doing well," he slurred. "I just lost me girlfriend. That's a Libra for you. I'm a Pisces." He leaned precipitously back on a chair and thought about the zodiac.

"Love is hell," I said.

"Aye, that's the truth," he said. "She's one of the forest people. I shoulda known better."

I looked to Eileen. "*Forest people*?"

She explained that the Forest of Dean is occupied by a real-life, honest-to-goodness clan. They don't communicate with the other people in the area, and they certainly don't like outsiders coming into their forest to date their daughters.

I called it a night and retired to my spacious, three-bed room. Wind and rain whipped the dark windows. I lit a candle and turned on the old black-and-white television. There were only five stations, one of which was Publicom. It's entirely in Welsh. I watched an hour of church congregation singing Welsh hymns before my eyes slowly shut.

november 4

. . .

BREAKFAST WAS SERVED on a lace tablecloth at a large oaken table in the bay window of the dining room, overlooking a garden. I was surrounded by statues and sculptures. It turns out that Eileen's son is a sculptor.

I paid her, took a few apples for the road, and said goodbye.

Chepstow Castle is an oblong structure built on the River Wye. It was the earliest stone castle in Britain, begun in 1077. The Chepstowians—is that a word?—added to it nearly every century for the next seven hundred years, so it's a hodgepodge of architecture.

Then Lady Fortune spun her wheel, and it landed on The Shaft. Through no fault of my own, I missed my coach to Swansea. Granted, it only cost me six pounds, but still, I was forced to wait for a train that departed much later. Onboard I sat next to a nice woman and her daughter. I offered them apples. They politely declined.

On the train, something was feeling a little bit off, a little weird, and I couldn't put my finger on it. Then it hit me—I hadn't seen any fast-food joints for two days. American cultural imperialism hasn't infected southern Wales just yet.

Then, not more than an hour later in Swansea, poetic justice laid down her card. When I asked a passerby how to get to the bus station, she told me to go "past the McDonalds and hang a right."

That evening, I eventually made my way down to the Gower Peninsula, to a seaside resort known as the Mumbles. It's known for its hang-gliding, windsurfing, and pub crawls. A favorite pastime of U of Swansea students on weekend nights is to "do the Mumbles mile"—one pint at each of the ten pubs lined up on the road along the harbor. I bet the town was named after how most of them sound after drinking ten pints of beer.

I began to sense that Americans are barely tolerated by the Welsh. This, therefore, was the perfect time to test out my Oxfordshire accent, which requires complete concentration. I don't always have that. My first victim was a fellow at a takeout place. As I tried to order a hamburger using a bungled British inflection, he narrowed his eyes as me. Whatever. I guess you can't expect too much from a place where people traditionally beat their lovers with wooden spoons. If that's how they treat *each other*, I'm relieved to still have my scalp.

My bed and breakfast is an immaculately clean joint run by a very open-minded couple. It's a good thing I found them. They have the only available single in town, it seems.

november 5

. . .

I ATE A THICK, greasy, authentic English breakfast this morning. Fried eggs, sausages, bacon, hash browns, baked beans, toast, and half a grilled tomato. Coffee and juice.

With me was an Australian couple who had been sleeping in the room next to me. Their teenage son is studying abroad in Nebraska. The man sniffled a lot and spoke haltingly in a sardonic tone. We tried to make breakfast conversation, but it was awkward.

With the ball of food and grease firmly planted in my stomach, I set off on my hike along the south coast of the Gower Peninsula. The coastal trail hugged the side of a mountain and tracked across several secluded beaches and small summer resort towns. The southwesterly wind whipped and cracked in my ears. Waves crashed upon the rocks far below me. Shafts of sunlight broke through rectangular windows in the cloud cover, looking not unlike one of those soppy, pseudo-spiritual Christian postcards that say, *"Walk while you have the light, lest darkness come on you; for he that walks in darkness knows not where he goes"* –John 12:35.

I ate my lunch on the side of a mountain in the crook of a rock. Then I entered the Bishop's Wood, where there was a tenth-century Anglo-Saxon church and hermitage named St. Peter's. It was a thick forest, nothing marked, not even trails. I never would have found it had I not encountered an old Welshman who was leading a British family.

"You're an American?" he said.

"Yes," I replied.

He pulled his pipe out of his mouth and squinted at me. "I thought you chaps all wore big hats and smoked cigars."

"No," I replied, "those are Texans. They're kind of like Americans, though."

I joined his followers, and the old fellow led all of us to the ruins, which were nothing more than an arch with some rubble roughly in the shape of a rectangle. There was also an ancient well nearby.

I spotted another Welshman nearby, working on his knees, trying to replicate an Anglo-Saxon hut using modern materials. Somehow corkboard siding and aluminum struts doesn't strike me as authentic.

I left the woods, and at the westernmost point on my long coastal ramble, I discovered a tiny hamlet. It was a smattering of four houses clustered around a single driveway on a secluded beach. I climbed onto a natural rock formation that jettied out into the sea.

That was the ten-mile point. It would be dark in under three hours. My brain was on automatic pilot and my legs felt invincible. I could walk ten more miles, or a hundred more, with no effort. Still, I decided to turn around.

———

Back in the Mumbles, I learned that it was Guy Fawkes' Day. I've never known when Guy Fawkes' Day was, but there was no missing it tonight.

Standing on the pier at eight o'clock this evening, I watched fireworks being set off left and right over the ocean.

The families were crowded around the launch site on the pier as though watching a juggler or a fire-eater. They seem to have no sense of self-preservation.

And the fireworks were really big. Local crazies shot whizzers and starbursts and bottle rockets right over the heads of the crowd from their spots on the mountain adjoining the beach. It was a little like being in a battle zone with Scuds and patriots and MiGs flying back and forth.

Through a series of events too complicated to relate, I found myself later at a nearby pub, ordering beers with a group of young Welsh teenagers. They were only fifteen years old, but they were drinking me under the table. It turns out that Wales is the kind of place where, as long as you can see over the bar, you can get served. In the States I would've been contributing to the delinquency of minors. Here I was being polite.

They were a cool group of kids. We discussed important social issues such as the success of the Cranberries, the universal appeal of *Baywatch*, and our favorite moments in *Jurassic Park*. I would've hung out with them for real, had they been in the States.

Leaving the pub, I thought about my upcoming birthday. I'm a week away from leaving my teens forever.

november 6

. . .

THE OWNERS of the bed and breakfast gave me a lift to the bus station. Nondescript travelling the rest of the day.

I did have fun trying to read Welsh, though. For future entertainment and edification, here are two street signs that I saw in Swansea, each in English and Welsh.

High Street
Strd Fawr

Have you paid and displayed your ticket?
Ydych chi wedi talu a dangos eich tocyn?

The Welsh language has 29 letters. The extras are *ll*, *ch*, and some other double-letter combo. Over twenty percent of the population still speaks it, though the teenagers last night rolled their eyes when I asked about Publicom. The language definitely isn't cool. In fact, I saw a newspaper headline featuring a quotation from a local leader saying that Southern Wales should stop trying so hard to hold onto its old culture and start forging ahead with a new one.

I think he's right. The Welsh clothing in particular is hopelessly tacky and needs a lot of help. On the street yesterday, I saw a man wearing a plaid shirt, pinstriped pants, orange socks, running shoes, purple gloves, and a black beret. This is extreme, but not totally unusual.

There are other gaudy offenses too. People seem to bathe in perfume and cologne. You can smell a gang of college students at least five minutes before you see them. A string of primary-color Christmas lights permanently lines the seaside road, lending it a carnival tent atmosphere. And then, most heinous of all, Mumbles has imported some palm trees and planted them in the town square. It looks about as disharmonious as a penguin in the Florida Everglades.

But what else can you expect, really, from a town whose name is derived from the Viking word for *breasts*? It was named after the two large mounds jutting out of the water just south of town.

On my last stop, a bus connection in Newport, I had an eerie, spooky, stiff-hair-on-the-neck type of psychic occurrence. Wandering around the city for an hour or two, I found myself singing the song "Love Shack" under my breath. No idea why. It's one of many songs that comes galloping unbidden into my mind and out of my mouth, but this time it seemed to stick around a lot longer than most.

I turned a corner at the north end of town and suddenly found myself staring at a pub named the B-52s.

november 8

· · ·

HAVING VERY few set classes each week and a whole town full of pubs is tough on the ole alcohol intake. Perhaps I know I'm developing a problem when, faced with nothing to do for twenty minutes before my tutorial, I head into the Lamb and Flag for a quick pint. It was Thomas Hardy's favorite pub, I rationalize, the place where he wrote *Jude the Obscure*. However, being buzzed on a glass of Boddington's does not help one discuss Shakespeare's so-called problem plays, I can tell you.

Yesterday at Keble College, while waiting for dinner, I noticed a familiar-looking girl at the bar. She had spoken at a debate on pornography. She'd delivered the standard conservative morality-is-not-created-in-a-vacuum speech. I remembered that she was an American, so I knew she'd be more open to talk than the British students.

I sat down next to her at the soup table, looked over, and said, "You're that libertarian girl from the Union."

"Not really libertarian," she replied, "though I do love Ayn Rand."

We talked. She'd just been rejected by all ten of the top ten law schools in the United States. She's reapplying after she finishes a quasi-graduate program at Keble this year. She did her undergrad at Yale. Reassuring words from her: Yale examines the whole package, not just the grade point average. Frightening words, too: their American Studies program is the strongest in the nation. Maybe I'll rethink that plan.

november 11

• • •

THE HEIGHT OF IRONY: I woke up on my twentieth birthday with a new zit on my face. When will it ever end?

I treated myself to a tour of small pleasures, ending with a pickle and some olives at a deli. Then I paid a visit to Narek at the sandwich shop where he's working, explored Magdalen College, and watched a rugby game at Christ Church Meadows.

Rugby is a primitive sport. Part of me wants to say that only lesser evolved men like to play it. But you can't tell just by looking at the players—they all could pass as J Crew models, at least here at Oxford ... their preppiness, their height, and their hair ... always the hair, flopping against their heads, hands running through it, smoothing, patting, stroking. Of course the illusion is shattered when one of them falls in a scrum and the others step on his face.

That evening, I and ten others decided to head to a pub on the outskirts of Oxford for dinner. The taxicab ride was a bit like Mr. Toad's Wild Ride, with us sitting in a small boxy black cab, bouncing through a dark road and seeing a little English cottage looming in the headlight—*we'd better slow down*—thatch roof and goose door ornament—*we're going to hit it!*—and the taxicab making a sudden perpendicular turn a mere half-second before barreling through the front doorstep.

The pub was called The Trout, and it was situated next to a small waterfall on the Thames. It was a long, low-slung affair, with a pub at one end and a bar at the other. Everything was wooden tables and medieval slate underfoot and hearths roaring orange with well-stoked fires. And despite all this, it was dead at seven p.m. on a Saturday night, as dead as that small bird you find in the corner of your garage during spring cleaning.

Accompanying us was Dr. Joseph Monroe, an English professor visiting from Hillsdale College. He made us, almost with gun to our temples, talk about our respective colleges. I stammered something along the lines of how my home university does the sex-drugs-rock'n'roll thing as well as anybody. Not really, since it's such a conservative institution.

My friends must have felt sorry for me that nobody was remembering my birthday, because a piece of Funky Monkey chocolate cake appeared before me, with the group's melody ringing in my ears. Then came a slew of Beastie Boys impressions. Happy birthday to me.

Back in Oxford, I attempted to play snooker at the Union. British snooker is an odd arrangement: fifteen red balls, six colored balls, and a white cue ball. The table had probably twice the square footage as a typical billiards table back home. It felt like shooting pool on a putting green.

november 12

. . .

CAROL and I grew more than a little irritated by the towering stack of dirty dishes slowly fusing themselves together in the shared kitchen sink. We rolled up our sleeves and with the do-gooder spirit of altruism began to wash and dry other people's dishes. I cleaned nearly 70 pieces of silver-ware alone.

Truth be told, the only reason I spent an hour doing these dishes was so that I could write a scathing self-righteous note and tack it to the kitchen door.

november 13

. . .

AMANDA and I watched an episode of *Amazing Stories* on BBC. Mary Stuart Masterson and Christopher Lloyd starred. Previous to that, I watched a documentary on Churchill with Kevin. Being a war buff, he's a good one to watch that with.

V-1 flying missiles were so slow, he said, that Allied fighter pilots used to save ammunition by flying alongside them and tipping them over with their wingtips. V-2s were much faster, though.

Watching the screen, I suddenly realized that an entire generation of Americans has no idea what it's like to live in a wartime situation. No ducking, no cowering, no ration cards, no bomb shelters.

"That's why we're a bunch of pansy-asses," Kevin helpfully offered.

What would Miami's South Beach do if an armada of Cuban warships anchored half a mile out? Squirt Coppertone? Hide under the lifeguard station? Rollerblade into a hotel lobby to wait it out?

november 14

• • •

I LEARNED some interesting facts today.

Chariots of Fire is the top-grossing movie in Britain, ever, period. *ET* comes in eighth.

The Bodleian Library is the largest in Britain, with over 5 million volumes. Compare that with Harvard Library, which has more than 11 million.

Ronald Reagan delivered a speech at Keble College in 1991. For much of the two hours, he spoke about jellybeans. The dons were livid, but Ronnie rambled on, oblivious. Occasionally, they say, he forayed into a bit of foreign policy, but continued to return to jellybeans, stating his special love for the red ones. This was a man who had his finger on *the button* only three years earlier. Scary.

The housekeepers who make up the rooms on my floor are a jolly lot. Two young women and an old man. They fuss, gab, and titter for five hours every day. I wonder how efficient they really are, though. Once I witnessed all three circled around a bag of garbage, attempting to move it in three different directions at once.

The old man, Skip, has proven to be a constant source of entertainment for the last two months. He is always talking to himself, always extremely apologetic, and always cheerful. This earned him the nickname Happy Guy Housekeeper, until we found out his name was Skip, which is funny enough on its own.

Skip has the strange habit of saying "No worries" in response to just about everything. It's a greeting, a farewell, and everything in between. I once overheard him say, "No worries. Nope, not me—why worry? No need to, no worries."

He'd always struck me as a bit of a neurotic, until I found out the truth this afternoon.

Apparently Skip had been part of the D-Day beachhead invasion at Normandy.

He *survived D-Day*.

He really has no worries.

a note from the author

. . .

THE PERIOD from November 14 to December 1 was marked by nothing except cranium strain. I worked every day, spent a lot of time alone, and have come to dread Keble College Library. Thank you for your understanding the lack of entries.

december 2

. . .

MISFRENCHOPY: hatred of French people

Of all the times to host a railway strike, they do it *now*. All the French railroads are shut down. I'm scheduled to go to Rome for the Christmas holidays, but to get there, I now have to bypass that great big worthless hunk of Western European real estate.

Why are the French living right *there,* in the middle of Europe? Should they be off somewhere in isolation, like, say, Sakhalin or Madagascar?

The railway strike is apparently getting violent too. That's scary. I study history, I know what happens when the French start to rebel against themselves. The idea of French internal warfare is even more frightening today—heavily armed military snoots plugging lead into anything that even looks remotely American. I hope EuroDisney is heavily fortified.

But I'm still pissed off. Shouldn't a more *welcoming* people be living where the French are now? A group of people who smoke a bit less and who, with penetrating insight, see Jerry Lewis for the goofball he is? Someone, like, say, Betty White.

She's welcoming. In fact, let's round up all geriatric Florida retirees into a series of cargo planes and airdrop them at various scattered points around France so that they can't band together and get back. Meanwhile, we'll move all the actual French to Guam, because the U.S. kind of owns it, and it's isolated. We'll float baguettes and wine over there once in a while, and maybe a spare Lewis movie once in a while.

Tonight, Kevin opened up about himself. It started out good, but quickly spiraled down into a *bona fida* Eeyore glum woe-is-me speech about his life. First he said that the people who speak their mind in America are prosecuted. I think he meant *persecuted*. Second, he explained why King College—which he recently transferred away from—was such a frustrating, bash-skull-on-granite kind of place. The archconservative student body, all Ralph Reedites, spent many hours lecturing him on the Bible's absolutism. They warned him that evolution was a horrible, evil, twisted lie dreamed up by the sinful press. They also solemnly informed him that Jesus believes in free markets.

Divine sanction given to capitalists. That's … interesting. King College seems to have inherited none of William Jenning Bryan's politics—but all of his hot air.

december 3

. . .

"I consider postmodern cinema to be the bogus imposition of our Western cultural hegemony in an act of indefensible neo-colonialism."

−attributed to Keanu Reeves

THIS AFTERNOON, I knew that something, or someone, was drawing me towards Blackwells, the best bookstore in Oxford, for I watched my legs and feet pump vigorously towards the inconspicuous doorway next to The White Horse.

But oddly enough, the Great Hand of Gonzo steered me past the main entrance, towards a second door that I never use. I pushed inside and, voila, there it sat on the table directly in front of the doors.

The new P.J. O'Rourke book.

It's called *Age and Guile beat Youth, Innocence, and a Bad Haircut*. It was in high company, sitting there beside a new biography of W.H. Auden. The famous poet's face on the dust jacket, by the way, is lined with so many creases and folds that he resembles a Sharpei, or a four-month-old brown sack lunch that I found at the bottom of my locker in high school.

So I've been reading that O'Rourke book all day, trying to avoid thinking about my up-in-the-air train journey to Italy.

And trying not think about leaving Oxford University.

december 5

. . .

I PACKED for a little while in the afternoon until the sun came out. Then I roved around Oxford one last time, pulling in the sights, sounds, and feelings, bidding goodbye to its ancient brick and stone as one might shake the hand of an old friend. Down High Street, across the Radcliffe Camera, in front of Blackwell's, New College Lane—the mere thought of leaving conjures up a poignancy that puts an ache in my stomach and tears in the corners of my eyes.

The last seminar with Alastair was somewhat less moving. We yakked about everything and nothing for ninety minutes. He even let me go and move my laundry from washer to dryer. At the end, I took my final paper back from him, stood up, spun around, and left without a word. There just didn't seem to be much to say, I guess.

In the evening, Makenna and I walked to the King's Arms for a final pint. White snowflakes whirled around in the inky black of the night sky. The Sheldonian loomed to our right and glided past us. It was like living a movie, really, seeing all of Oxford glide by like that. I threw my scarf over my shoulder and dug my hands deep into my pockets.

Standing in the pub with a pint of Winter Warmer, I

looked at the ruddy faces laughing and drinking, and I felt a sensation that I will call "instant nostalgia". It was the briefest realization—only a second long—that everything will continue without me. The cheerful imbibing, the camaraderie. I am but a mere blip on the Oxford radar screen, a transient here in this town, in this country, in this hemisphere. There have been many others before me who were far greater; there will be many more even greater. I was allowed to be a small part of this place for a few months, and I will carry in my heart forever.

Makenna returns from the bathroom and my glimpse into the rose garden ends. We empty our glasses and walked out the door with nary a second glance. Back at our building, I bid farewell to several friends, my mouth making empty promises that I'll write soon.

We've all trickled off to bed now, and here I sit with an empty desk and a suitcase, making this last entry.

I am missing Oxford only now that I am preparing to leave it.

plotworks publishing

If you enjoyed this book, please leave a review where you purchased it.

Then visit Plotworks Publishing to browse our many original titles and classics reprints. Sign up for our newsletter and get a free book!

more by j.a. jernay

Turn the page for a free peek at another title by J.A. Jernay: *Advice From a Former Digital Nomad*!

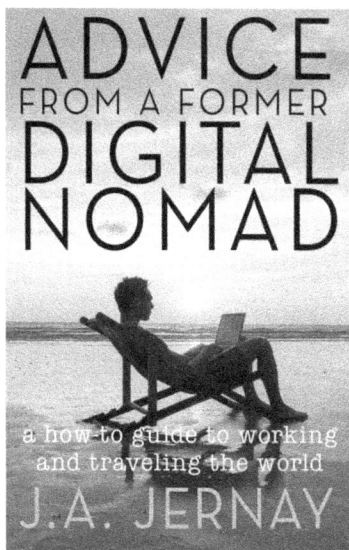

advice from a former digital nomad

She was respectful, responsible, diligent, and pretty. She was a practical choice for a life partner, at least on paper.

The problem was that she routinely worked sixty to eighty hours per week. It left almost zero time for us as a couple, and she didn't particularly care. I registered my displeasure, but there was no saving the relationship. She didn't *want* to save it. She just wanted to be left alone to work, period.

The workaholic had also decided to purchase a new condo. She invited me to give up my apartment and move into her new place, which was a sign of sunnier skies ahead. So I rolled the dice, trusting in her usually good judgment. I downsized, selling half of my furniture on Facebook Marketplace.

In retrospect, selling a lot of my furniture was an excellent decision. I had also sold my car the year before (in Chicago, they're not necessary), another good decision. I'd accidentally set the stage for digital nomadism.

So, in May of 2020, I found myself in a Tribeca-style open-floor-plan loft in the Lincoln Park neighborhood of Chicago. It was the start of the pandemic, and we were living and working together in a single large room. In other words, we were on top of each other, and with no end in sight. The workaholic began viewing me resentfully, as an obstacle to her efficiency.

In July 2020, I ended the relationship. There was some obligatory yelling, but the workaholic found a pebble of self-awareness and accepted it. For the next few nights, I lay there on the couch, thinking about my next move.

In March, I'd been visiting Riyadh and Dubai as the first wave of the coronavirus pandemic began, and barely made it out before they closed the airports. The epidemiologists said that another wave was on its way that winter, and it would be worse due to the cold weather. A vaccine was still at least nine months away, they said. The winter holidays, still half a year away, would undoubtedly be cancelled.

I would very shortly be homeless, and I'd sold two-thirds of my furniture. If I wanted to reestablish myself, I'd be in for a long, cold, lonely winter in a semi-furnished Chicago apartment.

Then my mind turned to politics. I'd watched the BLM marches plunge straight down Halsted Street that summer, thousands of people spontaneously assembling via Twitter. Thoughts of 1968 danced through my mind, and I worried about what was else was coming down the pike that November, especially given the 2020 presidential election. After all, we'd elected The Joker to national office, a psychopathic con artist in orange clown makeup. I was worried that he might stir up the populace in a never-before-seen way, and that things might get violent.

In short, between breakups, disease, politics, and civil unrest, U.S. cities weren't looking too attractive. It would be a good time to get out for a while.

Next, I looked at my work. Outside of my writing, the pandemic had helped me pick up many new clients in my freelance career as a freelance academic counselor, private tutor, and curriculum subject matter expert. Prior to the virus, half of my work had been online. Six months later, it had all gone online, and more was being added every week. I was suddenly doing really well.

Then I took stock of my personal life. There were a lot of things I didn't have, for better or for worse, things that other people my age had willingly pursued. I owned no home, always preferring renting for its flexibility. I no longer owned a car. I no longer had a girlfriend or a wife. I had no children, to the best of my knowledge. I had no need to take care of my parents, who were elderly but independent. My extended family and friends didn't depend on me for anything either, except for messages and emails and phone calls and funny stories. I had some credit card debt, but the balances were low.

In short, there wasn't a lot tying me down anywhere.

Then I took stock of the things I *did* have. I was enjoying a rapidly growing income. The pandemic was arbitrarily lifting certain sectors of the economy while destroying others, and I'd been one of the lucky ones. As a freelancer, I knew that my employers and clients didn't give two drips of runny shit where I lay my head at night. I was free to go anywhere I wanted, as long as there was dependable wifi.

Then there was the medical consideration. I've always enjoyed excellent health, part from luck and part from habit. This mattered a lot in a virus-driven pandemic that took delight in killing people with comorbidities. The official IFR (Infection Fatality Rate) for my age cohort was about 1-in-450. That of course was massively overestimated, since it only counted documented cases of covid-19, and we know that millions of people recovered alone, at home, without any official record of their illness. The real denominator in that ratio was likely quadrupled the official estimate, so the chances of me needing medical care anywhere in the world was very small.

(That said, if I'd been obese, or immunocompromised, or

afflicted with metabolic syndrome, I never would've left the US. I would've absolutely stayed close to home and top-notch medical facilities.)

Furthermore, I had built fluency in Spanish. For five years, the workaholic and I had spoken Spanish together, socialized in Spanish, and traveled in Spanish. I'd even started understanding her Catalan as well. This had made traveling in Latin America, and Spain, much easier than it ever been before.

Most of all, I harbored a strong desire to explore the world. It's a big place, and we should go see it all. Check out my other titles, if you don't believe me.

In short, I was free to leave—if I wanted.

I had set up a series of dominoes in my life, some on purpose, some by accident. Now the universe had added a few more. A global pandemic, the spread of broadband, and a new videoconference application called Zoom. All of this made a remote working life possible. All of these things made the concept of a digital nomad life possible. People were already doing it. I'd read about them, always from the safety of my couch.

All I needed to do was touch the first domino. But first I needed to admit to myself that I *wanted* to do this.

I breathed out, looked at the ceiling, and made my final decision.

Yes.

I would become a digital nomad.

plotworks publishing

Visit Plotworks Publishing to browse and purchase our many original titles and classics reprints. Sign up for our newsletter and get a free book!